TOUR FEVER

The Armchair Cyclist's Guide to the Tour de France

J. P. PARTLAND

A Perigee Book

The Berkley Publishing Group
Published by the Penguin Group
Penguin Group (USA) Inc.
375 Hudson Street, New York, New York 10014, USA
Penguin Group (Canada), 90 Eglinton Avenue, Suite 700, Toronto, Ontario M4P 2Y3, Canada (a division of Pearson Penguin Canada Inc.)
Penguin Books Ltd., 80 Strand, London WC2R 0RL, England
Penguin Group (Ireland), 25 St. Stephen's Green, Dublin 2, Ireland (a division of Penguin Books Ltd.)
Penguin Group (Australia), 250 Camberwell Road, Camberwell, Victoria 3124, Australia (a division of Pearson Australia Group Pty. Ltd.)
Penguin Books India Pvt. Ltd., 11 Community Centre, Panchsheel Park, New Delhi—110 017, India
Penguin Group (NZ), cnr. Airborne and Rosedale Roads, Albany, Auckland 1310, New Zealand (a division of Pearson New Zealand Ltd.)
Penguin Books (South Africa) (Pty.) Ltd., 24 Sturdee Avenue, Rosebank, Johannesburg 2196, South Africa

Penguin Books Ltd., Registered Offices: 80 Strand, London WC2R 0RL, England

Text design by Tiffany Estreicher
Cover design by Ben Gibson
Cover photograph by AP/Wide World Photos

PRINTING HISTORY
Perigee trade paperback edition / May 2006

PERIGEE is a registered trademark of Penguin Group (USA) Inc.
The "P" design is a trademark belonging to Penguin Group (USA) Inc.

Library of Congress Cataloging-in-Publication Data

Partland, J. P., 1968–
Tour fever : the armchair cyclist's guide to the Tour de France / by J. P. Partland
p. cm.
ISBN 0-399-53255-2
1. Tour de France (Bicycle race) I. Title.

GV1049.2.T68P37 2006
796.6'20944—dc22

2005055236

PRINTED IN THE UNITED STATES OF AMERICA

10 9 8 7 6 5 4 3 2 1

DEDICATION

To family, friends, acquaintances, and passersby whom I overwhelmed with bike racing minutie: thanks for tolerating.

ACKNOWLEDGMENTS

Much like winning the Tour, it takes a team to produce a book. While I don't want to rely too heavily on sports metaphors, it is an apt one. While my name is on the cover, a number of people toiled to see my words make it to these printed pages. My wife Beth not only lived with stacks of books and piles of printouts on the floor, and requests for help formatting, but accepted my going to France in the summer for "research" with good cheer. My parents and siblings were always there when I needed them. Jeff Kellogg found the publisher. Lars Klove, John Verheul, and Eric Rosenthal functioned as extra eyes. On the Perigee end, Michelle Howry and Meg Leder edited and put up with my incessant queries and suggestions. To publisher John Duff, vice president of paperback sales Patrick Nolan, cover designer Ben Gibson, and managing editor Kim Koren, thank you. Thanks are also due to the people I interviewed for this book. I asked plenty, and hounded (nicely, I hope) until they acquiesced. I could not have finished the book without them.

CONTENTS

PREFACE

Compared to how Americans learn ball and stick sports, we learn bike racing backwards. For baseball, basketball, football, hockey, and to a lesser degree golf, skiing, and tennis, we're immersed in the culture of the sport before we are conscious of it. Before we learn language, we are plunked down in the midst of people talking about America's big sports; we hear it in passing, we glance at the scores in the newspaper, we see the clips on the evening news, we see people wearing the uniforms and fanwear and carrying the gear. We understand the cultural context of certain sports because they're in the bath of American society. Look at the generational divide in soccer. Everyone who grew up playing it is comfortable with the sport, while most of those who were introduced to it because their kids played still don't know exactly how it works or why people care.

Most Americans approach bike racing in general and the Tour in particular with barely any context. Many of us rode bikes as kids, but we used them to transport us to the baseball game, rather than riding our bikes as the objective of the activity. We don't learn bike racing in gym class. Thanks to Lance Armstrong, you may know a cyclist, but few are friendly with a racer, and fewer still have seen a race in person. It's no wonder watching or reading about the Tour is a frustrating experience.

The Tour can be maddening to the outsider. Not only is there so much to understand, but the sport is simply different than any other. The race is different than most races, and there's a sizeable language barrier—even when discussing the race in English. This shouldn't be surprising. If a foreigner watched the biggest sports in America having had no prior exposure or explanation, it would be equally bewildering.

My introduction to the Tour was confusing but fascinating. When I was five or six, my mother read the story *The Big Loop* to me. It is the story of a boy who dreams about riding the Tour. It was romantic and exotic; most everyone was poor and worked hard. Fathers were missing because they had been in the Resistance; a boring teacher came alive when discussing his days as a racer. I didn't understand everything, but at that age not understanding everything is normal.

When I was in seventh grade, on my bike, I started racing cars downhill to school and racing friends uphill home. It was fun, but I was looking for ways to get stronger and make my bike faster, looking around at bike information. I had heard that an American was set to ride the Tour. That American, Jonathan Boyer, led a mythically difficult life. Word had it he lived in a closet in his team's headquarters when he first started racing in Europe, had nearly died from a crash, used acupuncture to recuperate from training, spoke fluent French, was called Jacques, and few even knew he was American. He was on the team of French great Bernard Hinault, and his job was to help Hinault in the mountains. I had no idea what any of this meant, but I liked the idea of riding insanely long distances through all sorts of conditions. The few pictures I saw of the Tour showed people with intense stares, beautiful bikes, and crazy outfits, riding frighteningly close to one another through incredible places. Exotic, romantic, brutal, epic; all good.

I had to know more. Whenever someone dressed like a European bike racer—I didn't even know there were bike races in the United States—passed on the road, I tried to follow them. It must have amused the cyclists; a kid on a clunky, too big, 40-pound bike trying to keep up. Over the years, I've likely become that cyclist.

With this book, my hope is to provide context for the Tour. I've broken down the world of the race into its most basic elements, and once they are introduced and explained, have added more complex elements, until you can understand and enjoy the race not as an outsider, but as a fan—as if you grew up with the Tour around you, a racer in the family, with a few trips to see the Tour pass through your region, and maybe even a chance meeting of Anquetil or Merckx.

INTRODUCTION

The Tour de France is more than just a bicycle ride around the country. It's even more than the pinnacle of bicycle racing. It's a spectacle that reaches far beyond France—a three-week-long soap opera experienced around the world.

When Lance Armstrong crashed on the final climb to Luz-Ardiden during the 15th stage of the 2003 Tour de France, a gasp was heard around the world. Seconds could have been lost, and those seconds could have decided the outcome of the race. People refer to Bobby Thomson's home run in the 1951 National League playoff game as "the shot heard 'round the world," but his home run was barely a sneeze in the forest compared to the frenzy of the Tour.

The collective gasp when Armstrong crashed wasn't just that of more than 2,000 journalists covering the race, nor the hundreds of thousands of fans lining the roads on this particular day of the Tour, nor the untold numbers who follow the Tour online, streaming the TV feed on their computers or following "play-by-play" coverage written and uploaded every few minutes to bike racing websites. There are also the millions who tune into the race on the radio and watch it on television on every continent and virtually every country on the planet. One-day races, or stages, within any Tour de France last between three and seven hours, and there are millions who follow every second of every stage. It is estimated that 20 million people attend the Tour every year. Some stages have crowds in the hundreds of thousands, often outnumbering the collective attendance for an entire seven-game World Series.

Cycling fanatics—*tifosi* in Italian—knew what Lance's crash meant. It was everything; the spill could have cost Armstrong the Tour. Armstrong had waited until the last climb of the last mountain stage to put his nearest competitor, Germany's Jan Ullrich of the Bianchi team, in difficulty. After two weeks of racing, Ullrich and Alexandre Vinokourov of Khazakstan and Team Deutsche Telekom had been his two closest challengers. After the Col du Tourmalet's brutal mountain climb earlier in the day, Vinokourov was out of contention. Ullrich was the only one who might be able to challenge Armstrong for the victory.

Even when it appears that a racer is dominating a three-week-long bicycle race, his lead can be both large and small at the same time. To be within 1 percent of the winner at the end of the Tour might seem impressive, but that often means being about fifty minutes—sometimes twenty-nine places—behind the winner.

Ullrich started Monday, July 21, 2003, fifteen seconds behind Armstrong, who had lost that much time in the crash. Armstrong had shown prowess on the climbing stages in the Alps, but had been beaten by more than a minute in the stage 12 time trial three days earlier, and he needed a time cushion in order to ensure his overall victory six days hence. There was another time trial in five days, and Armstrong would need to start the time trial with a one-minute lead in order to feel safe against Ullrich. Armstrong was the better climber and *should* have been able to outclimb his rival by over a minute on Luz-Ardiden . . . until the crash derailed his careful strategy. Being the better climber doesn't mean much when one is stranded at the side of the road with a non-working bicycle while the race keeps going.

No one was sure what Ullrich would do. Would he attack the fallen Armstrong? Would he wait? Ullrich himself was probably unsure. If he attacked, he might ride into the lead of the Tour, which wouldn't guarantee victory, but would give him an advantage. Even if he attacked, he might cramp or get caught or push himself too far and blow up, which would cost him the entire race. There was also a chance that Armstrong was hurt, and if so, Ullrich would be able to again ride away from Armstrong even if Armstrong could catch up.

Racing literally shoulder-to-shoulder at breakneck speeds calls for certain etiquette. Nobody really wants to take advantage of another rider's misfortune. Everyone acknowledges that chance is a factor in bike racing. As a result, in stage races, racers don't often deliberately attack a fallen rider, especially if he's in contention for overall victory. There is also the possibility that any victory one takes by attacking a fallen rival will forever cast a shadow over the victor. In an event followed by thousands of journalists and millions of fans, it can be a stigma that follows one's career.

Ultimately, Ullrich and the other leaders decided to call a truce on attacking and ceased their hostilities until Armstrong caught up. In 2001, Armstrong had waited when Ullrich crashed. This time, Armstrong caught up, took a breath, followed an attack, dropped the rider with him, and won the stage, setting up his overall victory.

This stage, like most of the 2003 Tour, was a nail-biter from start to finish. Cycling fans love this. Most sports fans appreciate close contests, but bike racing is not simple to explain to outsiders.

The simple definition of the Tour is this: It's a three-week bicycle race held annually in France. Comprised of 20 stages, it takes place over 23 days and covers a distance of around 2,100 miles, which leads to an average of around 100 miles a day. The racer with the lowest overall elapsed time is the winner. The race usually starts with 198 riders riding on 22 teams of 9 riders each. The most visible symbol of the Tour is the *maillot jaune*, the yellow jersey, which is worn by the race leader, the person with the lowest time. The Tour is supposed to provide a mix of difficulties (flat roads, hills, medium mountains, big mountains, winds, narrow roads, as well as solo and team races against the clock of varying terrain and distance), so that the winner is a "complete" rider who is smart, strong, fast, and most consistent.

For most outsiders, bike racing is as foreign as France: different names, different pronunciations, different customs. Kilometers instead of miles. Compounding the problem is that many Americans see a bicycle as a toy, as something easy, and have a hard time seeing athletes of moderate builds as particularly fit specimens when compared to athletes in our big three sports—baseball, basketball, and football. Further confusing matters is the fact that cycling is a team sport, even though each team rides as nine individuals.

This book endeavors to close the understanding gap. It will explain the Tour for the unique sporting spectacle that it is. Far from being an esoteric pursuit, the Tour is the second-most popular sporting event in the world. Only World Cup soccer has a larger audience. There are people who travel around France, "Deadhead-style," in a van and camp out beside the roads to watch the race pass every day. There are folks who follow the Tour via bicycle.

When Jonathan "Jacques" Boyer became the first

American to race the Tour in 1981, few Americans knew or cared. Many people didn't even realize he was an American. But U.S. coverage of the Tour got a boost in the mid-1980s, as Greg LeMond climbed to the top of the race and CBS aired the event on television. The bruising battles between LeMond and French legend Bernard Hinault, his teammate, made for great television and history, with LeMond finishing second in 1985 and winning in 1986, 1989, and 1990.

American cable sports television signed on in the 1990s. Even though LeMond was fading and fewer Americans were riding in the Tour, there were enough interested viewers that a race between Spaniards, Germans, Danes, Dutchmen, and Frenchmen was plenty interesting. Live coverage was unavailable, but half-hour to two-hour evening recaps became regular fare. Fans also started to get regular coverage in newspapers.

Everything changed when Lance Armstrong rode to—and then published—his own miraculous Tour story in 1999. With the Internet now a major news source, one can now follow the race online as well as on television and print. There is now live coverage of the Tour six days a week, with long rebroadcasts twice a day. Tour stages are covered on the evening news. Photos of the Tour have even made the front page of the *New York Times* on several occasions in the past several years.

With Armstrong's record-tying fifth Tour victory on the line coinciding with the 100th anniversary of the race, attention was magnified, both in the United States and around the world. The cyclists answered with an incredible race, filled with everything that bike racing offers: nail-bitingly close finishes with high-speed thrills and crashes, and the outcome of the race in the air until the end of the penultimate stage.

In 2004, Armstrong won a record-setting sixth victory. Lance and his team gave their best-ever Tour performance, dominating the race at every turn.

In 2005, Lance had a new team, was a year older, and his competition seemed to have gotten even better. Other teams started following Lance's blueprint and were building superteams as well. Some of his former teammates, having learned from the master, were leading rival squads in hopes of becoming the new Tour champ. The race should have been harder-fought and the finish even more closely contented. Despite having a relatively mediocre spring, Armstrong crushed all. He and his Discovery Channel Pro Cycling Team's iron grip on the race was only threatened once in three weeks. A cycling swansong that few are able to contemplate, let alone match.

2006 is the dawn of a new era. Without a dominant racer in the field, the race should be more open, with more riders taking chances to see if they can not only take the lead, but impose their own paradigm on the race. In many respects, the race, owing to the absence of the now-retired Armstrong, should be harder than ever. Hard racing is generally exciting, so the coming Tour should be a great one to watch. But the *tifosi* will tell you every Tour is a great Tour. It was great when Armstrong surprised the world with his first victory, and great when he did the expected and won his last. So it will be whether Italy's Ivan Basso takes a step up the podium, or Ullrich finally wins another, or if a dark horse has a stupendous July and dominates.

Welcome to le Tour de France.

Tour Fever

1

NATURALLY EPIC

Far from being a crazy idea, the Tour de France makes perfect sense. It came from particular circumstances at a certain time and place. And it grew from there, quite naturally, into the spectacle that it is today.

To the uninitiated, no sport makes any sense. Basketball? To quote a famous movie line, "What is so fascinating about a group of pituitary cases trying to stuff the ball through a hoop?" Football is an almost Sisyphean struggle of overgrown men pushing a ball back and forth on a grid. Baseball is a pastoral event that barely qualifies as exercise to some. Golf is simply walking around manicured greenspace, hitting a tiny ball into a small hole.

So why on earth would anyone want to ride a bicycle around France in the summer? And why would anyone care to watch? Of course, those who have "Tour fever" are quick to explain the attraction . . . and a large part of that fascination is found in the history behind the event.

The Original "Amazing Race"

Every true sports fan knows that the real allure of the competition isn't found simply in the rules of the game . . . it's in the history, the struggles, and the personalities that bring it to life. Superhuman feats have always been popular. Since at least as far back as *The Iliad*, people have enjoyed epic journeys. The Tour de France began in 1903 as the ultimate reality television show of its day.

Cycling was an extremely popular worldwide sport in 1903, and bicycle racing was huge—not only in Europe, but also all across North America and Australia. Bicycle racers were amongst the highest-paid professional athletes of the era—and, at least in the United States, remained so until baseball and Babe Ruth eclipsed them in the 1920s.

The United States was a driving force in the bike world—not only in terms of innovation and manufacture, but also as a source of the sport's popularity, especially when it came to bicycle racing. Interestingly, 1903 marked the beginning of the end of the bicycle's dominance in America.

Bicycles, particularly since the advent of the chain-drive, safety bicycle, and pneumatic tire—all three were together by 1888—were the ultimate form of exercise, transportation, recreation, and social statement of the 1880s into the twentieth century. Bicycles were the definition of modern, and they helped bring the world out of the Victorian era. They weren't cheap, but they were attainable. In the 1890s, American piano manufacturers were concerned that bike sales were eating into their business.

Bicycles were high-tech for their day, and they certainly brought change . . . but, in many respects, the world needed to catch up with bicycles. For one, roads in the late 1800s weren't generally paved, making cycling for long distances difficult. (Cyclists were among the earliest champions of paved roads, which, ironically, led to the popularity of cars, not bikes.) Bike companies stayed cutting edge for a long time, bringing innovation not only to bikes but also to industrial production in general, and to the world at large. Many bike companies became the pioneering forces behind airplane and automobile technology. The Wright Brothers were originally in the bike business, as were the Dodge Brothers. Albert Champion, the man behind AC sparkplugs, was once a top bike racer.

Bicycle racing had been around almost as long as bicycles, which many trace to the 1860s. Track racing in particular created international stars—the "Michael Jordans" of their day who were known and idolized the world over. And because racing preceded the Olympic movement, the "amateur" ideal championed by the Olympics was never really accepted by fans of competitive cycling, who saw professional contests as the apex of the sport.

Making and breaking records was in fashion, as it is now. A cyclist, "Mile-a Minute" Murphy, rode a mile in less than a minute behind a train in 1899. The hour record, the distance a solo rider can pedal on a track in sixty minutes, was already 40.781 km (25.48 miles) in 1903.

Besides the allure of high speeds over short distances, there was an appreciation of distance records. The first long-distance bike race is believed to have taken place in 1869. That race was Paris–Rouen, which was 134 km (83.75 miles), and was won in 10:25 for 8.05 mph average speed. Road racing between cities became popular in Europe. Races weren't short. The point of racing was to create an epic test of strength, fortitude, and technology. Then, as now, the extreme was championed. The first ultra-long-distance bicycle race, a race on the track that lasted six full days, took place in New York City's Madison Square Garden in 1891. Six-day bicycle races became popular and were contested for years. This was also the first year of Paris–Brest–Paris. At 750 miles in length, it was France's ultimate endurance bike race.

Bicycle races were often organized with an interest in commerce. Bicycle manufacturers liked races because they promoted bike sales, and newspaper companies frequently organized races to sell papers. While there is now a chicken-and-egg quality to it, many of these races are still around today, and are still associated with newspapers. The Tour is still linked to *L'Équipe*, the Giro d'Italia is still linked to *La Gazetta Dello Sport*. The Het Volk classic in Belgium is promoted by the *Het Volk* newspaper. The Dauphine Libere stage race is promoted by the newspaper of the same name, though the Dauphine race is a good bit newer than the other races.

The First Tour de France

In 1903, the newspaper *L'Auto* was looking for a publicity stunt to sell newspapers. (Briefly known as *L'Auto-Vélo*, the sports newspaper had to change the name because the owners of competing cycling newspaper *Le Vélo* sued.) *L'Auto*, while a sports paper, owed its existence to the political climate of the day. Much of France was caught up in the Dreyfus affair.

Alfred Dreyfus was a French Army officer convicted of treason in 1894. At the time, it was suggested that his religion, Judaism, was the real reason he was convicted. Crusading journalist Emile Zola proved this in 1898, only to see Dreyfus convicted again in 1899. It caused an uproar in France, one that wasn't quelled until Dreyfus's exoneration in 1906. People took sides and urged others to do the same.

Henri Desgrange, a journalist and former racer (he had briefly held the hour record), was an anti-Dreyfusard who took advantage of the day's political climate to get

L'Auto off the ground. He had worked at *Le Vélo*, but saw the paper's pro-Dreyfusard position as his opening. Desgrange found some anti-Dreyfusard advertisers who were equally frustrated with *Le Vélo*'s position, and got them to back his venture. *L'Auto-Vélo* was born, printed on yellow paper to distinguish it from the green pages of *Le Vélo*.

L'Auto was not an overnight success. Desgrange was losing money and the confidence of his investors, and needed something that would put his paper on the map. *Le Vélo* had promoted the Paris–Brest–Paris (PBP) bicycle race, so Desgrange's solution was to launch a bicycle race that outdid PBP many times over. Since PBP was popular, six-day track racing was popular, and multi-day auto races were starting to be held, Desgrange's top people suggested a six-stage event on the road that visited France's big cities, in a circuit of France. It was a tour, an inspection, a geographic lesson, an experience of all France.

The idea of a Tour de France was hardly unfamiliar to the French of 1903. Many adults of the era had read in primary school a children's geography and history book entitled *Le Tour de la France par deux enfants*, in which two children travel around the country, visiting sights and getting to know the countryside as they journey to find their uncle. In fact, the idea has been traced as far back as the sixteenth century, when Charles IX went on a two-year tour de France to shore up political power and unify the country. And craftsmen of the early 20th century, as they had for a long time, engaged in a tour de France to learn the complexities of their trade. It has even been suggested that there is an agricultural history of making a loop on the edge of one's grounds to mark one's property—the Tour thus marks what is France.

The idea behind the race was simple. Start in Paris, and visit the major cities—Lyon, Marseille, Toulouse, Bordeaux, Nantes—and return to Paris. The cyclists would ride the entire distance from one city to the next. The fastest person after the six stages would be declared the winner. If someone couldn't finish one day, they could start the next, but were no longer in consideration for the overall prize.

The first Tour de France was beyond extreme. Nothing like it had ever been done; there was no way to know if a human body could stand the rigors of the event. The race distances were epic. The six stages were 476 km (297 miles), 374 km (233 miles), 423 km (264 miles), 268 km (167 miles), 394 km (246 miles), and 471 km (294 miles) in length. Roads were terrible. They started before dawn in the morning and rode through the day, until after sundown. The riders also had to be their own mechanics. They had to make all their repairs on the road themselves or risk being thrown out of the race. The only advantage they had was that they didn't race every day, as rest days were scheduled in between the stages.

But if the challenges of this first Tour were daunting, the spoils were great. The overall winner of the race got 3,000 francs, which has been estimated as 1,200 days' pay for the average French worker of the time. The first Tour finished with tangible proof that it was a success. Twenty thousand people filled the Parc de Princes velodrome in Paris to witness Maurice Garin race onto the track and win both the ultimate stage and the inaugural Tour de France. Of the sixty starters, twenty-one finished.

For *L'Auto*, the race was a success as well. The paper printed 130,000 copies for the final stage of the race, which is said to be an increase of 100,000 over their normal circulation. Further, it helped destroy their competitor, *Le Vélo*, which went out of business by the end of the year.

Desgrange and the Tour

In 1904, the race already showed some distressing side effects of its huge popularity. Racers were attacked on the road by fans of their rivals. It has been suggested that some of the roadside attacks, which were reported to be both violent and amounting to taking racers hostage, were the result of wagers made on the outcome. Many racers were disciplined for cheating, and the top three finishers, led by returning champion Garin, were thrown out of the race. The race craziness led even Desgrange to believe that the 1904 Tour was the last.

All the same, Desgrange saw scandal as a good thing. No sooner were the top finishers of the second Tour disqualified than he called for a third Tour. And the third had the first-ever mountain climb in the Tour. The climb was the Ballon d'Alsace, outside of Nancy. Could anyone climb it without dismounting? Insane. Brutal. Turned out it was typical.

Desgrange, while seemingly genius at creating, modifying, and marketing his race, was somewhat of an idea thief, taking the good ones presented to him and claiming them as his own. He was also something of a megalomaniac and sadist. It has been said that his idea of a perfect Tour is one where only one rider finishes; the flip side to this harsh vision is that every finisher has performed a heroic deed merely by completing the race.

As the Tour went on, it became apparent that Desgrange always wanted everyone to know that it was his race and he called all the shots. He also wanted the race to be brutally hard—the harder, the better. Even though bicycles of the time were already being equipped with freewheels so cyclists could coast downhill, Desgrange refused to allow them in his race for years. His repeated rationale was that taking advantage of new technology would make the race too easy. Later, he banned derailleurs on the same grounds.

He likewise didn't want racers swapping wheels or using other people's bikes. He hated teams. In 1906, Emile Georget, a popular racer, damaged his bike in a crash and took his teammate's bike and continued racing. This was a violation of the rules, but his popularity convinced Desgrange to keep him in the race. While the element of sponsored racers only grew as the Tour evolved, Desgrange preferred the independent riders, known as the *touristes-routiers* or *coureurs isolés*. For many years, this group had their own competition within the Tour.

One way in which Desgrange exerted his influence was over bike sponsors. He thought bicycle companies were ruining his race. Yes, it was ironic, but no matter. To lessen their influence, and have the race entirely decided on the merits of the riders themselves, he made all the riders cycle on identical, unlabeled frames in 1908. However, he failed to take into account other sponsors. Wobler tires offered a prize for the highest-placed rider who used their tires. The second-place rider won the Wobler prize and a generous bonus on top of his winnings. This battle regarding sponsors was not over for a long, long time.

The term *domestique* has been common usage in racing seemingly forever. It refers to a house servant, someone who works in service of someone else. Desgrange was the first person to use the term, and he meant it as an insult to a racer who sold his services so others could win. Desgrange thought such a person was unworthy of competing in his race, though he did allow them to start.

Desgrange also liked to demonstrate his grip on the race. One famous incident dealt with Eugène Christophe, who broke his fork on a mountain stage in 1913. At the time, the Frenchman was a favorite to win. Not only did Christophe carry his bike to the nearest town, but he tracked down a local blacksmith and forged the repair himself. Despite having done all this work, he was penalized ten minutes for allowing a boy to use bellows to keep the fire going. Later, the fine was reduced to three minutes. Christophe, a popular favorite, had bad luck follow him through the Tour. He also broke forks during two other Tours.

Frenchman Henri Pélissier, winner of the Tour in 1923, had an ongoing feud with Desgrange. Pélissier felt Desgrange had many stupid rules, and Desgrange liked using those rules to penalize Pélissier. In 1924, although the defending champion, Pélissier dropped out of the Tour with his teammates in protest. Desgrange was going to fine Pélissier for starting a stage wearing two jerseys and discarding one along the route. The resulting newspaper story, written by crusading political journalist Albert Londres, was titled, "Forçats de la Route," Prisoners (or Convict Laborers) of the Road, people submitting to be members of a chain gang, and the expression has stayed with the Tour.

Evolution

The next several years after 1905 saw the race starting to evolve. Stage lengths were shortened while the number of stages increased. The result was an increase in distance. To discourage cheating on the open road, time classification was replaced by a points classification in 1905. This meant that there was no difference between winning by a little and winning by a lot. It also probably helped further the concept of team-oriented racing. Time-based racing returned in 1913, when it was felt that the points system made for dull racing.

Desgrange wasn't above tinkering with his race if it meant adding excitement to it. He tried banning bike sponsors, meaning everyone had to ride official Tour bikes without logos. He saw the rise of team racing and tried to limit it by switching entries from trade teams, those sponsored by businesses, to national teams, those sponsored by national racing federations, in 1930. He added the mountains competition in 1933. After Desgrange's death, the promoters kept his spirit of tinkering alive, adding and subtracting elements when they were concerned about the popularity of the race, or the race becoming too hard or easy.

Eventually, mechanical assistance on the road was allowed in the 1950s, while national teams were discarded in 1962 in favor of trade teams. More competitions were added. Stages were shortened further. A prologue was eventually added. In time, the Tour visited every country neighboring France, even starting as far east as Berlin, as far west as Dublin, as far south as Spain, and as far north as the Netherlands.

The Mountains

Owing to both bicycles and roads of the era, riding up mountains was not part of the first two tours. When it was suggested as a test for the 1905 Tour, Desgrange was first opposed, then changed his mind . . . and then took credit for the innovation.

The Ballon d'Alsace, in the Vosges Mountains, was the first major climb of any Tour. Many believed people couldn't ride the whole ascent. And many didn't. But Desgrange liked the new obstacle and it stayed. In 1906, the first true Alpine climb, the Col de Porte, in the Chartreuse Massif outside Grenoble, was scaled. The mountains were to become ever more important to the Tour's identity.

In January, 1910, Desgrange sent an assistant to scout the Pyrenees for truly high mountain passes. The assistant took a train to the Pyrenees, hired a driver and asked him to drive up the Col du Tourmalet. At a certain point, the road was blocked by snow. The scout got out and climbed up on foot. While he had to be rescued, he told Desgrange the climb was fine. The Tour also paid for the road to be repaired, as they eventually did for many mountain roads. The 1910 tour had a stage that took in the Col de Peyresourde, Col d'Aspin, Tourmalet, and Col d'Aubisque. When this stage was added, no one was sure what would happen. The first high mountain climb that year was over the Col du Tourmalet. The second man over the summit, Octave Lapize, was pushing his bike. He yelled, "Murderers!" or, "Assassins!" at the officials standing on the road. He promised to quit the race. Then, he mounted his bike and rode down to the finish of the stage . . . and to win the Tour. Riders claimed to hate the change and went so far as to call the stage that encompassed all the climbs the "circle of death," which became another term to stick with the race.

The addition of mountain climbing called for changes in the bikes. Even though freewheels had been around for several years, Tour competitors were riding fixed-gear bikes, essentially track bicycles with a hand brake for the front wheel. This meant they had two gears for all conditions and could never stop pedaling. Each side of the rear hub had a cog on it, and the rider had to stop, take the rear wheel out, turn it around, put it back in, and then get on the bike and go. Freewheels allowed cyclists to keep their feet on the pedals, while the bike was moving and legs weren't. To today's thinking, this was an improvement that probably didn't make the race too easy. After the mountains became a race feature, freewheels were allowed.

Covering the Tour

Desgrange not only exercised tight control on the competition, but also on the media covering his race. The rationale was that the race should only benefit *his* newspaper. He didn't allow other newspapers to follow his race until 1922, and even then, he made sure *L'Auto* had more journalists than anyone else.

As the race progressed and technology improved, coverage got better. Radio coverage arrived in 1929, though the difficulties of driving and broadcasting made the work difficult, if not often impossible. In 1932 radio broadcasts began in earnest, though the reports were recorded and then broadcast after the stage finish rather than being broadcast live.

Regular television coverage of the race began in 1952, at a time when a home television was a luxury. The images weren't live, but broadcast on the following day. Live broadcasting began in 1959. The Tour started broadcasting beyond Europe in the 1980s, and was on the Internet by 1995.

As time went on the number of journalists covering the race grew and grew. The press corps now numbers in the thousands—approximately 2,300 journalists in 2005.

World Wars

In the history of the race, little has proved to stop the Tour. Impassable roads, snow, striking workers, and striking cyclists have all shortened stages. But to cancel the race, it takes a world war. The 1914 Tour began on the day many believe World War I started, the day of Archduke Franz Ferdinand's assassination. The 1914 Tour was completed, but didn't ride again until 1919.

The 1940 Tour was cancelled due to the Nazi occupation; the race didn't run again until 1947. Jacques Goddet, editor-in-chief of *L'Auto*, having taken over the Tour from Desgrange in 1936, refused to hold the race because of the Nazi occupation, calling the Tour "peace in July." This stance, while noble, was not the whole story. *L'Auto* continued to publish during the Nazi occupation, and was closed by the government upon liberation in

1944, accused of printing Nazi literature. Goddet opened *L'Équipe* (*The Team*) literally across the street.

The Modern Tour

Many separate the history of the Tour into two parts: the early days, from 1903 to 1939; and the modern Tour, from 1947 through the present. There could be many reasons for this. Bike technology moved forward, roads were better, training became more sophisticated, racers became faster. But it seems that the real reasons have to do with the impact of two things: World War II and media technology.

World War II so devastated Europe that everything that came after was considered a rebirth. Probably equally important is that after 1947, televised images of the race started being broadcast. And maybe people were looking for good news, and a way to reconnect with their past. The Tour could have been both modern and traditional. Goddet, in his manifesto that introduced *L'Équipe*, said that the paper was a calling to all that is noble in people. The Tour was an extension of this belief.

To many, the 1950s represent the height of the Tour's greatness. Those who followed the Tour since then seem to believe there are no heroes, no personalities like there were back then. Postwar rebirth, the novelty of TV, and longer vacations that enabled more French to see the Tour in person, probably all played a part, and maybe, like in the United States, a baby boom helped things along, as these Tours were the first in many memories of today's old hands.

In some cases, it could have been the great stories, including several legendary rivalries, that made the races and the champions memorable. Many sporting events have dramatic qualities—weaving the drama and the people who act in it is a natural fit for any storyteller.

That a bike race can last three weeks only enhances the drama, and often the race is told as a soap opera. Recently retired race director Jean-Marie Leblance, who was both a racer and a journalist, has suggested that some of the drama from the pre-television era came from journalists adding fiction to their race reports. Likewise, it is possible that the saturation coverage today might reduce any sense that the racers are heroic.

While there are at least as many stories as there are riders in any given Tour, there are some stories that stand out above others. The winner of the 1948 Tour is one such memorable figure. Gino Bartali, the Italian who first won in 1938, was known as Gino the Pious. Winning Tours ten years apart certainly helped his stature, but so did fate. After 1948's stage 12, Bartali was in second place, some twenty minutes down. In Italy, the chairman of the Italian Communist party was gunned down. There was fear of unrest, civil war perhaps, but allegedly, the anger was held off long enough to listen to the exploits of the Italian rider on the radio, who nearly climbed into the lead the next day, and went on to win the Tour.

In 1949, Bartali's nemesis and teammate, Fausto Coppi, came to the fore and won his first Tour. The two were considered rivals, polar opposites, different visions of Italy. While Bartali was religious and from the countryside, Coppi was considered sophisticated and urban. It has been said that the Pope asked Coppi to end his affair with a married woman, so important was Coppi to Italy. Some still believe that Coppi was the *campionissimo* of *campionissimos*. Coppi won his second Tour in 1952, with the greastest margin of victory of any modern Tour—twenty-eight minutes. There was an air of tragedy about Coppi—delicate features, sad eyes, a marked contrast to the robust health that Bartali exuded—and he spent most of World War II in a prisoner of war camp in Africa. He died in 1960 from malaria, which he contracted while racing in North Africa.

Louison Bobet, the first champion to win three Tours in a row, had to win over internal divisions on his French national team for his first victory in 1953. His teammates initially refused to work for him. But he demonstrated his strength in the mountains and promised his winning to his teammates, both of which convinced them to ride for him.

No sooner did Bobet step back than Jacques Anquetil came forward. The first man to win five tours, he was praised for his style but allegedly not loved for his cold demeanor. On the one hand, when a young boy asked him how to prepare for a race, he replied, "With a good woman and a bottle of champagne." On the other, he was also known as "Monsieur Millimetre," for a reputation of riding no harder than necessary to win. In 1961, he took the *maillot jaune* on the first stage and held it for the rest of the race, a rare feat.

A rivalry that brought both men great notoriety was that between Anquetil and Raymond Poulidor. Much in the way of the difference between Bartali and Coppi, Poulidor, Poupou to his fans, was portrayed as the gregarious country peasant to Anquetil, the aloof playboy. Poulidor, in contrast to Anquetil's comment "no miner loves his pick," thought any day on the bike was easier than working the family farm. Poulidor, called the Eternal Second, finished the Tour in second place three times between his first Tour in 1962, and last in 1976. In both his first and last tours, he finished in third place; most impressively the 1976 result came at the age of forty. Poulidor is still singled out as one of the great Tour heroes.

Poulidor actually helped end the format of national teams racing in the Tour. He chose not to race the 1961 Tour because he didn't want to ride in support of Anquetil. But he wasn't the only top pro who skipped the race; more and more pros decided they preferred to honor their commitments to their trade teams rather than their national teams. As a result, there was a sense that the 1961 race didn't offer the best competitors, which hurt the race's stature and helped return the Tour to trade teams.

Poulidor's big chance should have occurred when Anquetil retired, but it wasn't to be. Anquetil helped a teammate, Lucien Aimar, into the lead of the 1966 Tour and then dropped out.

Then the Merckx era began. Belgian Eddy Merckx appeared, winning the 1969 Tour, as well as all the jersey competitions. Merckx, "the Cannibal," the second man to win five tours, is considered by many to be the greatest racer of all time. Even now, over a generation removed from his final days as a racer, there are still legends and jokes told testifying to his greatness. One such joke is thus: What's the difference between God and Eddy Merckx? Answer: Some days God wishes he was Merckx. He is famous for living a "religion of attack," and wearing down his rivals by riding them into the ground. He won just about all there is to win in pro racing, and won those races many times over. While Merckx won five Tours, from 1969 to 1974, he was pushed to his limit for a few of those victories, which helped humanize him and kept the race interesting. In 1975, gunning for his sixth victory, he was punched in the liver by a spectator while climbing Puy de Dôme, and later crashed and broke his cheekbone. He still finished second. His last Tour was 1977, when many felt he was a shadow of his old self; he finished sixth.

No sooner did Merckx's era end than Bernard Hinault's era began. Hinault, a pugnacious Frenchman called the Badger, had the elusive "panache" that so many race fans love. In fact, he might have had too much panache for some. Not only did he enjoy the aggressive aspects of racing, but he seemed to love it. If he could, he crushed rivals—something fans didn't always appreciate. Winning sometimes seemed secondary to breaking legs and spirits. Though he won five Tours, he finished his career with a hard-fought second place in the 1986 Tour. There, he battled his teammate, American Greg LeMond, through much of the race, and the competition between the two devastated the rest of the field. Fans often seem to have mixed feelings about champions, and this last defeat probably won Hinault more admiration than many of his victories.

Cycling Goes Global

LeMond's tour victory started another era. It began what many have called the "Mondialization" of cycling. Professional bicycle racing was dominated by Western Europeans for much of the twentieth century, but LeMond's first victory marked the start of the ascendance of non–Western Europeans into the pantheon of racing. A Frenchman hasn't won the Tour since Hinault's last victory in 1985, and not only have the winners come from the United States but also from Ireland and Denmark—countries not known for their racing. The smaller racing nations of Germany and Spain have also won Tours. Italian Marco Pantani's victory in 1998 has been the only recent victory of a "traditional" cycling power.

While outsiders had been making their way onto the European racing scene for a long time, the 1980s is when the outsiders found a place at the head of the pack. Americans, Australians, British, Canadians, Colombians, Irish, Mexicans, and New Zealanders made it to the front. And, with the fall of the Eastern Bloc, Eastern Europeans and western Asians, who had dominated amateur bike racing for a long time, started arriving at the top of the pro racing heap.

LeMond himself was a transforming figure, taking Hinault's lead. Hinault, despite his famed combative spirit, did not try to win every race he entered. He was happy focusing on objectives he set and ignoring all else—he was never a fan of Paris–Roubaix, a spring classic that qualifies as a monument of cycling, but he rode it to win in 1981, won, and then said it was a stupid race and he wasn't entering it again. LeMond, partially as a result of this influence and partially as a result of a hunting accident that nearly took his life in 1987, refined the principle to be "the Tour or nothing." Before the hunting accident, LeMond raced everything well. From 1989 on, LeMond seemed to employ the Tour or nothing strategy for his seasons. It's a philosophy that subsequent Tour champions seem to have emulated.

1989's Tour was one of the most memorable. Both LeMond and Laurent Fignon, champion in 1983 and 1984, had returned to top form. Both riders had been teammates of Hinault when they were neo-pros. LeMond's return was all the more miraculous because of his amazing recovery from his hunting accident just two years prior. The two swapped the lead a number of times over the course of the race, and the outcome was still in doubt on the final stage, a time trial from Versailles to Paris, set in honor of the two hundredth anniversary of the French Revolution. LeMond started the day in second place, and in less than fifteen miles, erased his fifty-second deficit, a miraculous feat considering Fignon was one of the top time trialists of the day, and won the Tour by *eight* seconds, the narrowest margin of victory ever.

When LeMond made his push for overall victory up the climb of Luz-Ardiden in the 1990 Tour, one rider stayed with him. Spaniard Miguel Induráin, lead domestique of 1988 Tour winner Pedro Delgado, followed LeMond up the mountain and won the stage ahead of LeMond. It was a sign Induráin was ready for more. No more supporting Delgado; Delgado would support Induráin. Induráin won the next five Tours, from 1991 to 1995. LeMond cracked on the stage in which Induráin took his first *maillot jaune*. LeMond finished seventh overall and then fought a long, slow decline of his career.

Induráin was known as a strong time trialist who followed wheels in the mountains. Not an exciting winner, riding in the way that Anquetil did, but without the seeming ego of the earlier winner. He never seemed to speak much to the press and rarely seemed to suffer. Induráin would take his winning margin in the time trials, then he'd let the climbers set the pace in the mountains, forcing them to attack each other in order to beat him.

In 1996, Induráin came to the Tour, and could finish no better than eighth overall. He retired shortly thereafter. He was deposed by Denmark's Bjarne Riis, who was also nearing the end of his career.

Riis was succeeded in 1997 by his German teammate on the Telekom team, Jan Ullrich. Ullrich, second in 1996, was seen as a future five-time champion, but largely thanks to Lance Armstrong, has managed four more second-place finishes. Some say he didn't prepare well enough, that he gained too much weight in the winter, but considering that he beat all other riders save one, it's hard to find fault with him.

Ullrich was beaten in 1998 by Marco Pantani, an Italian who many believe was inhabited by the spirit of Fausto Coppi. Pantani, dogged by bad luck, accusations of drug use, and suspensions, came back to animate the 2000 tour, but committed suicide in 2004.

The Armstrong Era

1999 began the Armstrong era. As with LeMond, his back-from-the-deathbed victory not only increased American but worldwide attention on the race.

Armstrong, like any other multitime Tour Champion, has had a strong influence on the race and racers. He focused on the Tour about as much as LeMond, though he added major reconnaissance work by climbing most of the demanding stages months ahead of the race, and seeming yearly refinement of gear and training. Because of his success, many of his closest competitors have tried to emulate elements of his training. And since the next racing generation has spent the last several years learning Armstrong's methods and success, the ways are bound to be used and modified in the future.

In some respects, Armstrong is different than the previous champions. In his first Tour, his "story" was even more compelling than any head-to-head competition with fellow riders. In 2000, Ullrich and Pantani returned, but neither seemed to have a chance against Armstrong until the final day in the mountains, where an emotional Pantani attacked early to throw Lance off his game. Armstrong was thrown, and he "bonked"—ran out of calories to burn—which resulted in a sudden inability to ride hard on the final climb of Joux Plane. It was Ullrich's only chance all Tour to make up time on Armstrong. Pantani dropped out that day.

2003 was easily the most exciting Tour of Armstrong's reign, and one of the most exciting in years. The outcome wasn't known until the final time trial on the penultimate day, when Armstrong rode well, and Ullrich destroyed his own chances by crashing in the rain.

No one knows where the Tour will turn next, or who will be leading the charge, but wherever it will go, it will build on all the earlier Tours. The institution is stronger than ever, and growing.

The Tour is extreme, of course. That it is beyond categorization is why people watch and talk about it, and try to imagine what it takes. The race is inhumanly tough and it got that way naturally. To simply dare to start the race is a major feat. Finishing puts every racer into a special category, one bold enough to start, strong and tough enough to finish the race of races. Every summer, like the swallows returning to San Juan Capistrano, the racers return, and the people turn out to marvel at the sight.

2

SCORING THE TOUR

The Tour de France is a stage race won on time. The racer with the lowest time at the end is the winner.

The races that comprise the Tour are called stages. There are usually 20 stages and a prologue, contested over a twenty-three-day period. The most important contest in the Tour is the general classification (gc). These are the standings in the hunt for the race championship.

Riders begin the race with the same overall elapsed time—zero hours, zero minutes, zero seconds, zero hundredths of a second. The moment a racer crosses the start line on the first day, he starts gaining time. The clock doesn't stop ticking until he crosses the finish line each day. After every stage, the total for the day's race is added to his total from the previous days.

At the end of each day, the standings are recalculated based on the stage times. The person with the lowest overall elapsed time to that point is awarded the *maillot jaune* (yellow jersey), the symbol of race leadership, and he wears yellow for the next stage. (The Tour takes this so seriously that no team is allowed to have yellow as the dominant color in their team uniform.) The next day the process is repeated, and there might be a new guy in yellow or the same rider may retain the yellow jersey. It is typical to see six or seven riders assume race leadership over the course of a Tour. After the final stage, the person with the lowest overall elapsed time is given a final yellow jersey and is declared the champion of the Tour. He's the person who rode the race the fastest.

Scoring

The nine racers on each team wear identical uniforms. Each rider has two numbers on the back pockets of his jersey for visual identification. His main bicycle also carries a number plate matching that on his jersey and a tiny transponder for faster electronic timing. Every finish is videotaped and timed simultaneously, so the race judges can watch the time as the riders cross the line. If the finish is on a flat road, speeds will be close to 40 mph, so the judges will watch the finish in slow motion over and over again until they get all the numbers down. They enter the number and time into a computer, and all the calculations are done quickly. After the first mountain stage, figuring out standings for the leaders gets easier as there are fewer racers in contention for overall victory and the time gaps between riders grow larger.

When the field finishes en masse, the entire field is awarded the same time as the winner. If two or more riders finish together, all the riders are given the same finishing time as the first person in their group. However, if there is more than a bike length separating one finisher from the next, the second finisher gets his own finishing time. While this might not seem like an important distinction, it can be if the entire field is split in two halves at the finish. If the separation is more than a bike length, all those behind the bike length get a time that is counted from the moment the winner crossed the finish line—and this could be several seconds.

Time's a Ticking

In the Tour, there are no time-outs, no two-minute warnings, almost no way the race will stop between each day's start and finish lines. The few times the clock has been stopped was for unforeseeable difficulties that made the racing unsafe. Rain doesn't cut it. Flooding does count—sometimes. Snow squalls won't stop it. A snowstorm might. Striking workers blocking the road or a train blocking a crossing may or may not.

If a rider crashes or flats or accidentally goes off course, there's no time for standing around; the racer must get going as quickly as possible. If it suddenly gets cold out, stopping to put on a jacket is generally a bad idea; putting it on while racing is usually essential. A full bladder may or may not call for stopping. It is for this reason racers have learned to do everything necessary while on a moving bike. They can change most of their clothes, including shoes, while riding. They eat and drink on the go. They can get their bikes adjusted while riding them. They relieve themselves while rolling; if it's the result of over-caffeination, it's common for teammates to push the rider midstream. They can even visit a medical car while racing along.

For the race leaders, every second does indeed count. If they're in the wrong place at the wrong time, they might miss the key attack of the race and lose any chance of victory. They don't want to chance losing minutes or even seconds while waiting for a broken wheel to be replaced.

For the riders struggling to stay in the race, every second counts as well. Each stage has a time cut. Generally, all the riders have to cross the line within 15 percent of the stage winner's finish time, though the gaps vary depending on the terrain, distance, and speed of the race. This imperative has been known to cause riders to cheat in small ways—hanging on to cars, accepting pushes up mountains from fans—in order to get to the finish on time. This sort of help is frowned upon but generally not penalized, so long as the riders aren't contenders.

There are a few allowances to the time cut rule. One is that if a rider crashes in the final three kilometers of a stage, he is given the finishing time of the riders he was with when he crashed, and is allowed as much time as he needs to finish the stage.

The other notable exception is when a rider finishes beyond the time cut, yet distinguishes himself with his effort to get to the finish. The judges often give special dispensations for sick and injured riders who, despite their diminished state, suffer on and on and still get to the finish line. Such beneficence often yields only a day's reprieve; the next day usually isn't any easier.

Stages

A stage is merely a race within a race. There are a few different kinds of races in the Tour. There is a prologue, usually two to three time trials, usually one team time trial, and the rest are road races.

Every Tour starts with a **prologue**. A prologue is a short time trial, less than eight kilometers (about five miles) long. A time trial is an event where each rider starts alone, and races all-out alone. Since no one can see anyone else's effort—riders start on the course separated from other competitors by two-minute intervals—the only solution is to ride all-out for the distance. The prologue creates a quick sort of the entire field and easily determine the standings for the first day of racing. Prologues are usually placed in urban areas to make for great spectator events.

Time trials (TT) can be much longer. In the Tour, time trials generally vary from forty to sixty kilometers (twenty-five to thirty-six miles). If the timed test goes up a mountain, they're typically much shorter, 20–40km.

In a **team time trial** (TTT), the entire team, all nine riders, start the course together. They ride together in a coordinated fashion to maximize speed through aerodynamic efficiency to get the fastest time. The tricky part of the TTT is that the finish time for the team is taken off the fifth rider. And every member of the team has to cross the line within the time cut in order to start the next day. Can a team ride with fewer than nine riders in a TTT? They can, if they have fewer than nine riders left in the race. All riders in the race have to start with their team. If a rider was forced to abandon before the TTT, he can't start the TTT.

Road races are the easiest to visualize. The entire field starts at once, races together, and the winner is the first person to cross the finish line. In the Tour, it is typical for the races to be in a point-to-point format, meaning they start in one place and race to another, though occasionally, they finish where they start—which is known as a circuit race.

With the exception of the prologue and the finish on the Champs Elysées in Paris, the Tour's stages change locations every year. In part, this is to present the racers with new and varied challenges. It also jiggers the race so it is as exciting as possible.

Competitions

Since racers are losing time every day, the race might become a snooze if both the riders and public were only paying attention to the race for *maillot jaune*. To have something for every cyclist and cycling fan, there are a plethora of competitions—the points competition, the mountains competition, the best young rider competition, the most aggressive rider competition, team general classification, and the Lanterne Rouge, the award given to the last-place finisher. And then there are some extra prizes, like the Henri Desgrange prize for the first rider to climb over the highest point in the Tour. In the 2003 Tour, they created a Centenaire prize for the riders who scored well on stages that finished in towns that hosted stages in the 1903 Tour. The riders competing for these prizes still have to finish within the time cut, but they don't have to confine their ambition to a high gc finish.

The extra competitions provide viewers with more reasons to watch or attend the Tour, even when it appears that the race victory is certain. The racers get the chance to win more money and notoriety. The sponsors of the competitions and the riders get their names in the press. And to keep everyone apprised of progress and happy with exposure, all competitions have results tallied daily, so there is always someone winning and others moving toward victory.

Some Tour fans follow specifically for the "lesser" competitions. There are people who appreciate the difficulty of competing in the points competition, or the beauty of watching climbers duke it out over steep alpine peaks.

The Points Competition The leader of this competition gets to wear the *maillot vert* (green jersey). Just like with the yellow jersey, the green jersey gets scored every day. Riders who win a stage get up to thirty-five points, depending on what kind of stage it is. Win a hot spot, or intermediate sprint, and the rider gets six points (four for second, two for third). Points are accumulated throughout the competition, and at the end of the day, the jersey is awarded anew. This competition can speed up races in the middle of long days and adds extra intrigue to massive field sprints.

Time bonuses are awarded for winning stages and hot spots. When the leader of the Tour is winning by only a few seconds, expect his rivals to try to win hot spots to gain on him. In early stages, the good sprinters can ride themselves into the lead this way.

The Mountains Competition The leader of this competition gets to wear the *maillot blanc et rouge*. Like the other jersey competitions, it is scored every day. As with the points competition, points are awarded for winning or placing, which means being the first or near the first over a finish line located at the top of a "categorized" ascent. Every categorized hill has points for the taking at the top. The tougher the climb, the more points are awarded. There are five categories of climbs, Category Four being the easiest, then Categories Three, Two, One, and Hors Category (HC) being the hardest. Category Four hills award five points to the winner and only give points three places deep (first, second, and third get points). HC is found atop the toughest mountains, and points are awarded in descending order to the first fifteen riders to climb the mountain.

The Best Young Rider Competition The leader of this timed competition gets to wear the *maillot blanc*. Only riders under twenty-five years of age are eligible. This competition helps identify the stars of the future.

The Most Aggressive Rider Competition This is known as combativity in the Tour, and this is the only competition based on subjective judgments. Every day, a rider wins the most aggressive rider award, based on points awarded by judges who watched the entire stage. The person who wins one day wears his race number in white on a red background (all other numbers are black numbers on a white background) the next day. At the end of the race, the Most Aggressive Rider is the one with the highest point total in this competition.

Team General Classification This is possibly the most confusing competition in the race. Every day, the top three finishers from each team have their time added together. The cumulative time is then compared to the top three finishers from every other team in the race, and a ranking for the day is created. The team with the lowest time wins the day. Every subsequent day, the top three finishers from each team have their time added together and added to the total for the previous days. Therefore, a team can lead the team gc, not have any riders high on individual gc, and not win any single day's team gc competition.

Unlike the other competitions mentioned, there is no distinctive clothing for the team leading this competition. They are, however, awarded little lion stuffed animals for each day they lead this competition. It is the symbol of Credit Lyonnais, the sponsor of this competition.

Lanterne Rouge This award, a red lantern, began as a joke and is a bit of a dubious distinction. The red lantern was originally found on the back of a train's caboose. Because the final finisher is at the end of the train, he is symbolically awarded this prize for bringing up the rear. Some years, the two racers lowest on general classification "compete" to be last, but it's usually a joke.

3

LES ÉQUIPES

It takes a team to win the Tour.

The 198 racers who line up at the start are among the best bicycle racers in the world, but few have a chance at overall victory.

This isn't a bad thing. There are many possible objectives for the racers. The differing interests create an atmosphere where each development in the race receives close scrutiny, from riders and spectators alike. Racers with different goals are often the basis for successful breakaways, and these often change the complexion of the race. (More on this in chapter 8.)

As in any "natural selection" scenario over three weeks, the strongest, fittest riders will ultimately separate themselves from the pack. A less obvious selecting factor is that only a little bad luck, a bad day, or a bad moment will drop someone from contention. Just forgetting to eat enough during one stage could spell disaster on that day or the next. A flat tire when the race is on the boil could mean never catching up that day, or having to dig so deep that there's little left for the next day.

Support Riders

Contrary to what it may look like, the Tour de France is not contested by 198 individuals; instead, it's raced by twenty-two teams of nine cyclists apiece. Each of those riders has a role to play, and for most, that role is in support of the team's best competitors. These riders are known as *domestiques* in much of the bike world.

The *domestiques*, *gregarios* in Italian, are sometimes reliable professionals who have reached their limits and are happy racing in support of another rider, but they can also be veteran riders who have already tasted glory, young up-and-comers in need of experience, or sometimes are even team leaders in other circumstances. Though the role has a lowly title, there is glory for these riders, too. They're often the ones most people see first because they're at the front of the race for a long time; they are toasted as an integral part of the team leader's success and their skill at helping others gets them into big races and big pay. Lance Armstrong once remarked that if a cycling team were a jersey, he'd only be the zipper.

Team Selection

The twenty-one or twenty-two teams are selected by the promoter of the race, the Amaury Sport Organization (ASO). The twenty highest-ranked professional cycling teams in the world are automatically invited. The final one or two are wild-card selections, and the promoter is given leeway to choose teams that will add interest to the race. Because the Tour is in France, French teams often get the nod over equally worthy teams from other nations.

The teams themselves are comprised of twenty to twenty-five riders who race throughout the year. Each team takes the nine riders who are in the best shape at the moment and fit with the team's strategy.

While based in particular countries, cycling teams have become increasingly international in flavor, unlike in previous eras when it was typical for an entire team to hail from the host country. To say that a team is from a certain country, the team's roster must have a majority of riders from that country, but increasingly, the star rider is a foreigner. Besides improving the quality of racing, the internationalization has the added benefit of generating more publicity for a team and the sponsor. The Italian team Lampre (a coffee machine maker) gets publicity in Austria because they have an Austrian rider. The French team Cofidis (a phone credit company) has an Australian leader, to both win races and extend brand recognition across to the Anglophone world.

Not all twenty-two teams are trying to win the Tour. They'd love to have a rider win the race, but not all teams are equally strong or have a rider who is capable of challenging for the victory. As a result, each team has a slightly different strategy. Yes, the riders will be trying to win something every day, but each rider will have a different goal and not all teams are riding to win every day, as we'll discuss later. Yes, if any team has an opportunity to win a stage and take the lead in one of the important competitions, they will go for it. A stage win can help insure that a rider has a contract for the next season and that the team has a sponsor for the next season. A day in the yellow jersey can make a rider's career.

With every prize comes money, and the teams always share the money. They usually share it equally, so there is no benefit for selfish behavior. There is an ethos of sacrificing oneself for the team, and the sharing of spoils enforces it. All for one and one for all for these musketeers. When American Andy Hampsten rode the Tour in 1986, he was having a great ride, sitting in fourth place and leading the best young rider competition, but two of his teammates, Hinault and LeMond, were battling each other for the victory, which seemed to take all of his teammates' attention. Hampsten flatted toward the end of a stage and was concerned that his teammates wouldn't notice him stranded by the side of the road as they raced by in the peloton. But they had; they waited and then helped him chase down the field because they had calculated the value of him winning the white jersey and finishing in fourth and knew what share they'd get of that money.

Cycling is a sport created out of capitalism, but where a socialist ethic reigns. Bike racing was initially promoted by bicycle companies to sell their goods to an unaware public. Racers quickly learned that sharing the prize purse was a good way to improve chances of victory, so they devised strategies where friends and associates could help one another win.

At the Tour, it is tradition that the winner renounces his share of the prize money, so his team can have more. It's a grand gesture that keeps *domestiques* loyal and acknowledges that a victory can mean hefty appearance fees at exhibition races and a better contract the next year. An extreme example is Lance Armstrong. He promised a $50,000 victory bonus to each of his teammates who rode the Tour with him. Making a year's salary in three weeks is enough to keep every member of Lance's team training hard and racing hard just to get on the Tour team.

Teams of Yellow Jersey Contenders

The *maillot jaune*, or yellow jersey, is the ultimate success symbol in cycling. As we discussed earlier, it is worn by the leader of the race, the person with the lowest overall elapsed time. Time is calculated at the end of each stage, and whoever has the lowest time is awarded the jersey and gets to wear it the next day. The racer wearing yellow after cumulative time is calculated at the end of the last stage is the champion of the tour.

The Discovery Channel Pro Cycling Team, Lance's team, is an example of what team composition is like for a serious contender. The entire team was built to help him win the race. His teammates were not looking for a high finish, or a stage win, or a day in yellow, but if those things happened and they could still support their leader in his quest for the yellow jersey, so much the better. The eight guys entered to support Lance were a combination of time trialists and mountain climbers. These riders were expected to protect him through the flat stages so he could save as much energy as possible and set the pace for him through most of the mountain stages to wear out his competitors.

Protecting a rider during flat stages means sheltering (hiding) him from the wind, from other riders, and keeping him near the front. Bike racing is partially about wind management, and "drafting" is a way to save as much as 50 percent of a rider's effort. A draft is the pocket of wind that a cyclist creates by riding. The faster the rider goes, the bigger the draft gets. Drafting is tucking behind another rider or a group of riders to save energy. The faster one goes, the more one can save energy by utilizing this technique. Riding solo at 25 mph is roughly equivalent to riding over 30 mph behind someone. And the effect is magnified as the pack gets larger. That saved effort adds up when a rider is cycling 100 miles a day for three weeks at an average speed of around 25 mph. Sheltering the protected rider saves his energy for the moments when he needs it.

Sheltering from other riders is also a way to promote the safety of the leader, as he knows his teammates won't get too close and risk crashing or try to nudge him into the wind in order to get better position. Keeping a leader near the "sharp end" (the front) of the race is the key—far enough from the front that they get draft off the lead riders, but close enough to the lead that they'll be able to avoid the crashes. Imagine driving a car bumper to bumper at breakneck speeds for four hours. If one person crashes, how many people would that take out? Being near the front is good positioning so the leader can race up the road with major attacks, but it is also essential for teams riding for the overall victory as it minimizes risks. No one wants to lose seconds or minutes, or see the leader abandon with a broken collarbone when the race is on "easy" terrain.

Support riders will also stop with the leader when he has a flat tire or another mechanical difficulty and wait to pace him back to the front of the race. Often one *domestique* will give up his own wheel—literally take it out of his bike and give it to the protected rider—so the leader can get back into action quicker. If the leader's bike is disabled, a *domestique* might even hand over his own bike. If the leader needs food or water, *domestiques* will give up their own supply or slow down, drop behind the race, get sustenance from the team car, then ride all-out to catch up with the leader and hand over the nutrients. They'll also stop or even literally push the leader when he has to heed the call of nature.

On flat stages, the bigger riders tend to spend more time helping the leader while the climbers, who are often smaller, try to save energy for the mountain stages. When the mountain stages come, the roles are reversed—big guys help out early, then fade to the back to rest up for another day.

Protecting a rider is more difficult in the mountains. One way to protect a team leader is by setting a fast pace uphill, a pace the leader can handle, but one that is difficult for other leaders to maintain and discourages the climbers, often referred to as mountain goats, from attacking. A steady, fast pace uphill is one that benefits riders in great shape. It slowly turns the screws on weaker riders and also prevents those already in difficulty from catching back on. A contender's team will try to use up their riders slowly in the mountains, keeping the pace high until the slopes of the final climb or two where, hopefully, the leader can attack his rivals and gain time.

But plans are just that and strategies change when the race is in motion. It isn't unusual for a Tour contender to get sick or injured or not ride up to expectations. They're human, and the task is almost inhuman. At this point, the team has to change its focus in order to salvage something. Sometimes, a support rider goes on a tear and finds himself elevated to team leader, like when Thomas Voeckler rode a long breakaway into the yellow jersey in 2004. He surprised everyone and led the race through the Pyrenees into the Alps. Other times, the team pursues another goal, like winning a particular stage or another jersey competition.

The Team of a Green Jersey Contender

The green jersey is worn by the leader of the points competition—points being awarded for finishing at the top of a stage or in a hot spot sprint. It is the second-most important category in the Tour. If a rider has proven himself a consistent enough sprinter to win this competition, it is typical for his team to be built for the objective of getting him as many points as possible.

A team in the hunt for the green doesn't need specialty climbers, but rather strong guys who are good at going to the front and setting up their sprinter for his final burst of speed. They have to be able to move their protected rider to the front of a pack charging in excess of thirty miles an hour and then ramp up the pace in the final kilometers.

They usually have a very good sprinter who starts his effort a bit early to slingshot the leader to victory.

These teams often save their energy in mountain and time trial stages to better battle on the flatter days. Another tactic of teams looking for the green jersey is to send out a rider on a long breakaway so that the other contenders lose the opportunity to gain points. For these teams, it doesn't matter whether the remaining riders finish thirtieth or 150th, so long as the protected rider wins the green jersey.

Winning points means winning and placing well in as many stages and intermediate sprints as possible. If the team leader doesn't have the stamina to go for all the sprints as often as possible, the team takes a fallback position of setting up their sprinter for stage victories.

The Team of a Polka-Dot Jersey Contender

The climber's jersey, white with red polka dots, is awarded to the rider with the most points scored on hilltops. Here, climbers with the ability to sprint over the summits of mountains are favored. The points awarded are also weighted in favor of the bigger hills, so some teams will try to have their top rider accrue points on the smaller hills, so he can go into the mountains with a cushion of points.

This kind of team stocks climbers, and their strategy tends to be the reverse of the green jersey teams. They hide in the pack on the flat stages, only making an effort when a breakaway is possible or a hill is approaching, and ride the time trials as easy as possible, conserving their efforts for when the road tilts up.

Here, too, when the leader falters, the team must create a plan B. Often it means a few riders focusing on winning one mountain stage, then a few riders focusing on another. It's fine for a rider from this team to win one day and finish last the next, so long as he isn't adversely impacting the team's goal.

The Team General Classification Contender

Team General Classification (Team GC) is most appreciated by the *tifosi*, possibly because it's hard to score and harder to explain. Every stage, the cumulative elapsed time of the first three riders to finish from each team is compared to the other top three riders from each team. The team with the lowest cumulative time is awarded the team prize for the day and that total is added up each day for the team general classification. Just like with the yellow jersey, the team with the lowest cumulative total at the end of the race is the winner.

Back in the day, the team leading this category wore yellow cycling caps during stages, making the Team GC leader easy to identify. But, as helmets have become mandatory in bike racing, the identifying marks are gone—so spectators need to be well-versed in the Tour to understand what's going on. A squad going for Team GC victory is made up of time trialists and climbers, as these are the kind of stages where major time differences occur. Each team needs to have at least three riders focused on doing well and going for victory on the days when time gaps get big. The others should be riding conservatively, making sure they're ready when it is their turn to attack.

The contenders for Team GC start to become apparent in the second week of the race, as the gaps start to get bigger. To secure victory in Paris, these teams often have to do well on the days when everyone is tired. When the racers are tired, they're content to let a breakaway filled with "unimportant" riders race away early and take the day's victory by up to twenty minutes.

At one time, the teams in contention for this prize were the same teams as the teams going for the yellow jersey. This has become less common as the yellow jersey teams are afraid of expending energy that they might need to protect their leader. However, teams of yellow jersey contenders are known to win the daily team race during some mountain stages and time trials.

Teams Without a Contender

The teams that come to the race without a clear favorite in any category hedge their bets. They bring their best sprinter, their best two or three climbers, possibly their best time trialist, and the rest of the team is there to help whomever is doing well. Should the leader(s) of the team falter at their assigned tasks, the support riders are given a more free hand to pursue their own goals. If these riders are feeling good and the stage characteristics suit their strengths, they can try to win the stage.

These teams will be happy with whatever success they can find. If they gain the yellow jersey early in the race, they might put all their efforts into holding onto it as long as possible. This will sap the strength of their climbers, but the possession of yellow for several days is a better bet than risking everything on a rider from another team getting lucky or riding above expectations.

If the team doesn't have any good climbers or standout sprinters, they'll come to the Tour looking for stage victories. These are opportunists, and they are the unknown quantity on just about every stage. It is typical for such teams to try to break away from the pack early in the stage to gain television time for their sponsor and try for the long-shot victory. This kind of team will always try to hold onto whatever lead they happen to get. Regardless of what it is, they will use all their resources to keep their lead as long as possible.

There are many pros who are at the top of the game but can't handle the three weeks of the Tour well. They try to pick their moments to shine. With 198 riders, there's a good chance that each stage favors some riders' talents over others.

These teams often get a helping hand from the teams looking to take the yellow jersey to Paris. The contending teams might want an easy day, so when they see a breakaway with low-placed riders from weaker teams, they might help the rider get up the road by setting a slow tempo at the front and discouraging other teams from chasing.

The Teams Behind the Teams

For every team in the race, there is a support staff that helps the riders get to the start line every day and cares for them during and after the race. The leader of this crew is the *directeur sportif* (d.s.). He manages a behind-the-scenes team that has become bigger than the team riding the race. It usually includes an assistant *directeur sportif*, four or more mechanics, and three or more *soigneurs* (helpers). The teams with better support will probably bring a doctor, a chef, and possibly a chiropractor. This team has two support cars in the caravan every stage of the race, as well as a bus to transport the riders, a truck for all the gear, and a few more cars to ferry the rest of the support staff.

The *directeur sportif* is the manager of the team. He directs the race strategy, gives the pep talks, tries to coax the best out of each of his riders. He's usually an ex-professional himself, and like managers in big-league sports in the United States, he has usually worked his way up the racing ladder. He probably directs the team's business interests and is the liaison to the sponsors. Some even own the company that manages the team—the sponsors usually just sign a big check over to the team at the start of the year and that ends their direct involvement with the team.

During every stage, the d.s. can be found in his team's first car, directing the action. Each cycling team has two cars in the caravan that immediately follows the race. They carry spare food, water, and gear for the riders and give the director a close view of the *peloton*. He has a race radio that tells him of developments in the race, and a radio to contact his riders in the field, often a dash-mounted television to watch the race, and a few cell phones to connect with the support staff in the feed zone and at the finish line. In the back seat sits a mechanic who can adjust bikes while hanging out the window of the moving car, hand out food, water, clothing, and sunglasses, and take in spare clothing and helmets. When a rider has a mechanical issue, the mechanic can rush out of the car and change out a wheel with a flat tire in ten seconds. If the problem is more serious, it will take him just a few more seconds to grab a bike off the roof, give it to the rider, and push him back into the race.

The assistant d.s. drives the second team car, with an identical setup. There are two cars and directors in case a rider from the team breaks away from the field or gets dropped. One car either goes ahead or drops back. The drivers have to have nerves of steel and incredible reflexes, as they are squeezing through small openings between vehicles, cyclists, and spectators on narrow roads.

There are more mechanics who drive the gear truck to each stage finish. With four mechanics, the crew can clean and overhaul each bike every day and manage the backup bikes and specialty bikes (each rider has at least three bikes at the Tour, while team leaders could have several more). They start working the moment the racer gets off his bike and have everything ready to go by the time the rider wants to climb aboard the next day.

Further behind the scenes, there are *soigneurs*. They start the day by preparing the food the riders are going to consume during the race, have snacks ready if the team is hungry before the start of the stage, give the riders a light leg rubdown before the stage starts, then they rush off to the feed zone, which is usually situated about halfway through the stage. At the feed zone, they wait for the riders to whiz by and grab musette bags while racing by, then they rush to the finish line. At the finish line, they'll start feeding the riders again and setting up a list of who gets a massage when. Usually, each team brings three *soigneurs*, each seeing the same three riders over the course of the race. Chiropractors are now starting to make appearances on Tour team support staffs as another layer of insurance for keeping the riders healthy.

The Tour stops in a new town every day and there's no guarantee that the food will be edible. A bad meal can mean anything from a mild taste turn-off to food poisoning, so the best teams have their own chef. It might just be nine people eating two meals a day, but as each rider can burn upwards of 9,000 calories on the longest days, there is a lot of work.

And the best-supported teams have even more staff along for the Tour. It is common for many teams to travel with publicists to work with the media and massage visiting dignitaries and sponsors.

Tour contenders sometimes have their own personal staff along for the race. Lance Armstrong brought a personal mechanic and two bodyguards. Bodyguards are uncommon, but personal mechanics for the top riders aren't. Others have their own *soigneur*. Armstrong might also be unique for having official groupies. Every member of the team, whether on or off a bike, contributes to the success of the squad. This is the biggest bike racing show on earth and everyone in the business wants to be a part of it. Just to be part of the chase on a team is sufficient to taste the glory.

4

THE RACER

Fans of every sport will tell you their athletes are the fittest, most skilled athletes on the planet. Naturally, the same is true about professional bike racers.

Racers starting the Tour are impressive physical specimens. They come in different shapes and sizes, ranging from five feet tall to 6′5″ with most in a range of "normal," but don't let their builds fool you. They're not crazy tall like basketball players, big like football or baseball players, beefy like skiers, or as skeletal as marathon runners. At first glance, they might not even arouse notice. Standing around in street clothes, they might look like underfed graduate students or people who have just returned from a grueling trip. They generally possess a sun- or wind-burned face, deep-set eyes, and hollowed cheeks. Even standing around in bike clothes, they might not arouse too much attention. They generally look skinny compared to the average person. Many, if seen in shorts, have thickish, well-defined legs, which seem a bit odd in comparison to their arms and torso, which generally seem underdeveloped. The caricature of bike racers in *The Triplets of Belleville* gives the right sense of their look.

Look carefully, really carefully, and you'll start to notice some differences that separate cyclists from other fit adults. Their skin is paper thin and muscles bulge out with every movement, no matter how small. Veins can be seen just under the skin's surface. Their skills become more apparent when you watch them climb a mountain and sprint for the finish line. The effort, particularly when standing on the pedals and thrashing their bikes, is extreme.

Watching top bike racers riding along, even racing at high speeds, doesn't necessarily impress, unless you simultaneously spy a speedometer or are trying to keep up. The position they maintain on their bikes is comfortable to them, so they might look relaxed even when riding at speeds few can obtain. Part of this is they've learned to focus their effort only on what helps turn over the pedals. And by appearing cool and calm, they might fool their opponents into thinking that they're doing fine . . . even when they're suffering. It doesn't help that most racers wear protective glasses, which both shields their eyes from airborne particles and from the inquisitive gaze of onlookers. And helmets further hide facial tics that might lead one to make inferences about level of effort.

Most of their physical prowess can't really be seen. These guys have resting pulses that range from thirty-three to forty-eight bpm, whereas normal is sixty to one hundred bpm. They can keep their heart rate a few beats below their max for over an hour at a time. They have huge lungs, which can process five liters of oxygen per minute, where sedentary people can process about half that quantity. Their hearts have probably been enlarged by all the riding. They carry around 5 percent body fat at Tour time, while many people who are pronounced "fit" carry 10 to 15 percent. And they have the ability to ride themselves to exhaustion and then do it again, day after day.

They can propel a bicycle in excess of forty mph for short bursts on flat roads, race over thirty mph solo for an hour, and average over twenty-four mph for the entire Tour. They can hurtle down a mountain at sixty mph, passing cars because the drivers just can't drive fast enough on the serpentine roads. They can ride literally elbow-to-elbow with two hundred racers riding thirty-five mph for hours on end, and they can do it on any road in any weather condition.

With the advent of more precise training metrics, there are even more specific ways to quantify what top cyclists do. With portable power meters, we have a much better sense of how strong one has to be to climb, sprint, or time trial with the best. To win a mountain stage of the Tour, it is estimated that one has to produce 6.5 watts per kilogram of body weight for the final climb, which usually takes place after over 100 miles of racing, and the mountain can take thirty to forty minutes to climb. Likewise, it has been determined that sprinters can put out in excess of 1,800 watts when sprinting for the finish of a stage. But this skill can't be seen; it can only be experienced. If you stand on the side of a flat road and witness the Tour coming by, it will be over in a flash—so fast you won't have time to consider what you just saw.

Coordination

What's hard to see on highlight reels is the racers' tremendous coordination and lightning-fast reflexes. These qualities are often seen as being limited to athletes who play with balls and pucks, but it takes skill to pilot a bicycle at sixty mph down a sinuous mountain road riding on tires that are less than an inch in diameter. And it takes a focused, calm individual to ride at thirty-five mph in a *peloton* where one is surrounded by other cyclists doing the same. Even climbing a mountain with spectators standing inches away is impressive. Jonathan Vaughters, an American who rode the Tour three times, says that a Tour rider must have the reflexes of a Formula One racecar driver: "If you don't, you'll never be able to run at the front of the field."

Imagine being in a crowd so dense that the person on your right and left are leaning on you, and the person in front is only an inch ahead of your front wheel, and the person in back only an inch behind your back wheel. Now do it on a bicycle. At thirty-five mph. In the rain. On rough roads. And then, when someone crashes right by you, you need to know, almost instantly, how you're going to avoid the crash.

And not only can they do all this, but they can drink, eat, change their clothes, and effect minor bicycle repairs while riding at speeds few people can attain when rested.

Suffering

Another thing that pro cyclists believe separates them from other cyclists—and in many cases, from other athletes—is their ability to suffer. Whether it's enjoying putting others in pain, taking the discomfort as a Zen exercise, or not minding the suffering, being able to keep on going for hours when not feeling good is an essential skill. Just like on the show *Survivor*, these guys have to be great at outlasting their opponents. The people who do the best are the people who are the best at squeezing every last drop of energy out of their bodies, who ignore the voice in their head commanding them to ease up. Andy Hampsten, the only American to win the Giro d'Italia, missed one Tour because he injured himself riding—he blacked out while motorpacing in preparation for the Tour and hit a traffic circle. His response to the incident was that if he couldn't go all-out while seeing double, it was pointless to start the Tour.

And not all the racers have an equal ability to suffer. Considering how small some of the gaps are at the end of the Tour, this ability could mean the difference between winning and not even being noticed. Vaughters believes, "Once you have all the abilities, it's how much you can suffer, how much you can keep your head in the game day after day."

Since there are no official time-outs in stage races, racers have to be concerned about every second. A moment's inattention can result in a season-ending spill. Crashing hurts, and the road rash can last for days, but the key is to get up quickly and keep going. Luckily, the shot of adrenaline received after smacking the ground is usually enough to help suppress the initial pain and get you back on the bike. After you catch the *peloton*, a doctor riding in a car immediately behind the pack can patch the wounds, provided the pace isn't hard.

It's not uncommon to see racers get up off the ground after breaking a collarbone, wrist, ankle, or hip, and get back on their bikes to race to the finish line. American Tyler Hamilton broke his collarbone at the end of the first stage of the 2003 tour. He not only finished the stage, and the race, but rode to fourth place, winning a stage along the way. Greg LeMond once dislocated a finger crashing during a stage in the 1990 Tour. He pulled the finger, got it back into the joint, and kept racing. He got second on that stage.

Things like fever, food poisoning, saddle sores, boils, diarrhea, and worse are dealt with as part of the experience. If a racer collapses from fatigue, heat exhaustion, or hypothermia after a stage is completed, he has enough time to recover well enough to race the next day. These things often merit dropping out of lesser races, but not the Tour.

And collapse is possible. When Stephen Roche was trying to stay in contention during the 1987 Tour, he closed a two-minute gap to race leader Pedro Delgado on the final mountain of the final mountain stage. But when he crossed the finish line, he passed out due to the thin mountain air. The effort was enough to put him in position to win the race a few days later. On the opposite side, Laurent Fignon lost the 1989 Tour to Greg LeMond during a time trial on the final day. Fignon, perhaps knowing he'd lost, collapsed after crossing the finish line.

Toughness is an essential quality for a bike racer. The guys in the Tour are amongst the toughest of the tough. Everyone has raced well in the worst weather imaginable, has crashed hard and gotten up, has been hospitalized for something, has been able to beat up on most other racers in most places around the world.

Gentlemen Racers

The nature of bike racing creates a different culture around the participants. While the racing can be cutthroat, the racers usually remain somewhere between polite and downright friendly with their rivals. Part of it is the fact that they have to race elbow-to-elbow for hours at a time over three weeks at a Grand Tour and see each other at races throughout the year. Part of it is the recognition that people switch teams frequently, and an opponent one season could be a teammate the next. And if the competitors hail from the same country, they could be on the same team for the world championships later in the season.

It also helps to cultivate allies in the *peloton*. Even if one racer can't help another, or doesn't have a reason to today, he might have a chance tomorrow.

Pro racers are often decent with the media and public as well. Part of it is they realize that their body, their presence, their words are advertising for the company that pays their bills, so it behooves them to be articulate and interesting whenever they can. Many have no doubt received "media training" from their teams. And at least for North Americans, they're aware how little attention they get at home, so the change from being anonymous at best (every cyclist in the United States has been treated as the reason some driver can't drive as fast as she wants, and has been run off the road or worse) to suddenly worthy of media interest is pretty exciting.

Jour Sans

Literally, "a day without." Idiomatically, it's said to mean "a day without pleasure." Racers often mean this to be a day when their body isn't responding and they lose several minutes as a result. One of the keys to winning the Tour is to not experience a *jour sans* during the race. "Bonking" (running out of energy) or crashing at an inopportune moment usually spells the end of the hopes of several racers every Tour. But bad luck is a part of racing, and maybe the best are the best because they are able to persevere through their day without better than the rest.

Shaven Legs

Yes, bicycle racers shave their legs. They've been doing it for a long, long time. No, it doesn't have to do with aerodynamics.

There is more than tradition behind the practice. Leg shaving allows primarily for three things. One is massage. Denuded legs are easier to massage, for both the *soigneur* and the cyclist. Pro racers get daily massages, if not during training periods, then around races. *Soigneurs* will massage their riders' legs every day during a race like the Tour, and the massages can last over an hour.

Hairless legs heal faster from road rash. Hair follicles carry not only sweat but dirt, and that dirt can be held next to the raw skin, which can lead to infections. And when the skin is healing, hair only slows down the healing process.

The third reason is that it's easier to apply creams and oils to hairless legs. Riders often put hot stuff, powerful counter-irritants stronger than Ben-Gay, on their legs when the weather is cool. They also add a layer of non-petroleum-based oil to keep the legs a bit warmer when it's wet and cold out.

Many who don't get daily massage still shave their legs for the other reasons. And there are plenty of people who don't race who shave out of tradition and vanity.

They Do WHAT on the Bike?

Racers have learned to do just about everything while riding a moving bicycle. Eating and drinking are normal and essential. They start with pockets full of food and two water bottles on their bikes. During the race, they pick up more bottles and food, and add or remove clothes when necessary. This isn't just removing arm warmers or leg warmers, but jackets, jerseys, and undershirts, and they have even been known to change shoes while riding. Shoe changing is much easier now that most shoes have Velcro straps instead of laces.

They also can affect minor repairs, and stop by the medical car to get a wound cleaned and bandaged.

And, since the average stage can take four hours to complete, racers are bound to have to heed the call of nature now and again. Passing fluid either necessitates a stop by the side of the road—something only done when others are stopping and the pace is easy—or going on the bike by moving to the side of the road, rolling up a shorts leg and shooting. For the latter maneuver, a teammate is often employed to steady the bike or rider by pushing. In terms of the other waste disposal, let's just say a description of the act has been called a "three-hatter."

Where Bike Racers Begin

It takes years of development to attain the skills and strength necessary to compete at the Tour. Most racers start riding and racing at a young age, usually in their teens. While many sports see their top athletes emerge in their late teens or early twenties, bicycle racers are expected to reach the peak of their abilities in their late twenties or early thirties.

At one time, the expected route to the pros included the Olympics. Start as an amateur, work one's way up until reaching the national team, possibly go to the Olympics, then turn pro. But, if the Olympics were years off, or a pro opportunity was offered, the Olympics could be forgotten, as the reward and prestige of racing as a pro was considered much greater.

Now that the Olympics are open to pros, bike racing has been reconfigured, and racers are turning pro at a younger age. The distinction between amateur and pro isn't as great as it used to be, and there's even a category for eighteen- to twenty-two-year-olds, formerly known as Espoir ("hopeful") but now simply called U23. This doesn't mean young pros are racing the big races young; they're professionals, but usually riding smaller races and developing as pros for a longer time.

Generally, Europeans start racing earlier than cyclists in other parts of the world because the sport is more entrenched there. On all continents, racing exists largely because there's a strong club system—small, independent, nonprofit entities that have a mission of creating racers and promoting racing—which provides infrastructure to the sport.

In Europe, bike racing culture has deep roots, while in the United States, bike racing is still considered "alternative." It is not uncommon for European cities and towns to have large cycling clubs that run their own teams and even manage a velodrome (bicycle track). The well-supported clubs can nurture a cyclist from the time she or he's a junior until he's a professional. They have coaches and bikes, so almost any kid who wants to try out racing can join, borrow a bike, and be instructed on the ways of the sport. The bigger clubs often have a relationship with a professional cycling team, and the club acts as a farm system for that team.

In contrast, the American scene is barely organized. Most people start by buying their own bikes and learning the sport on their own. While the learning curve has gotten less steep due to cycling's increased popularity and the growing number of books and websites devoted to the sport, most American racers start out on their own and coach themselves. They generally jump from small club to small club as they get better and move up through the ranks, eventually turning pro. Some pick up a mentor or personal coach along the way; some don't.

Still, many regions of the United States have racing twice a weekend and at least once during the week for much of the racing season (which can start as early as January, as late as March, and wind through October, depending on where one lives). One of the difficulties of moving from racing regionally to nationally in the United States is that the country is so big, which requires lots of travel. Those who want to make the jump to national-level racing try to have their best form when the national racing calendar events show up in their region. Any more necessitates a grueling life on the road where one lives out of a car and eats road food for way too long, knowing that the bad food, unfamiliar beds, and poor rest will compromise one's skills eventually.

It's assumed in Europe that young racers who are serious about becoming pro are racing full-time once they're old enough to do so. While many Americans in the sport's U.S. governing body agree with this mind-set, there are still many racers who go to college and race at the collegiate level in addition to racing on the national scene. Interestingly, colleges often have teams large enough and old enough to have gear to loan out and coaches who help out, though it's often on a volunteer, ad hoc basis. American Tour contender Tyler Hamilton graduated from college before pursuing cycling full-time.

Most of the Americans who race full-time in Europe started by dipping a toe in the shark-infested European waters. Europe is different because there are a greater number of riders racing more races in a smaller geographic area. Just like street basketball in New York City, the concentration of competition helps everyone improve.

Some cyclists go over to Europe on their own; many of these racers go to the Flanders region of Belgium, where the racing is plentiful, hard, and there are minimal barriers for foreigners. In Flanders, the races are close enough together that most are riding distance from one another, entry fees are only a few dollars, and the prize lists are pretty deep; it also doesn't hurt that many locals are multilingual and can communicate in English. Some go to Europe at the invitation of the U.S. National Team, either staying at the team facility in Belgium or going to races around Europe. Some wrangle an invite to a European club, though these generally take political connections as well as racing skill. And a few go over for short spells with their American team.

Racing in Europe is hard for outsiders. The language, food, weather, and customs are all different, so not only is the racing difficult, but living often presents difficulties as well. For outsiders, more than half the struggle of racing well in Europe is feeling comfortable far away from home—a big deal when rest and recovery are the yang to the yin of racing hard. For many, the question isn't whether or not they'll get really sick, but when, and what to do when that happens.

Most people have to win to move up to better teams, to the pros, and finally to the top of the pro ranks. Winning gets people noticed, and works in many ways. Besides a kind of guarantee that someone is good, it adds a publicity angle when the person shows up to a race or gets mentioned in race reports.

Ranked

Another important aspect of results is they can figure into one's ranking. And that ranking affects every team. The Union Cycliste International (UCI, international governing body of cycling) ranks races in terms of importance. The more important the race, the higher the ranking; the Tour gets the highest ranking, while many races aren't big enough to get a ranking at all. The ranking determines the number of points the winner gets, and also determines the number of points those finishing behind the winner get. The rider's points work for both individual and team rankings. And being that the racing season runs from January into November, the points from any race disappear from totals a year after the race was finished, so there is little resting on laurels.

The points are important because teams want racers with points. They're interested in creating or maintaining a high team ranking, to assure entry into the biggest, most visible races, so maintaining a high points total is a form of job security for both riders and their teams.

To even start the Tour, not only does one have to be on a Pro Tour team, the highest division, but be one of the nine riders selected by the team to race. Many are itching to go because it is the biggest, hardest race in the world, while others are just as happy not to go for that same reason. It's more suffering than some want to deal with.

Racing Season

The professional racing season starts in January and runs though November or December. In that time, there are races on every continent, save Antarctica. Because of time constraints (and physical limitations!), it is impossible for riders to compete in every race.

Within the pro season, there is a calendar of top races that are open first to the top teams, and then by invitation. The top races are part of something called the Pro Tour, and it runs from March through October. Comprising the Pro Tour are races known as semi-classics (well-known one-day races), classics (the toughest one-day races), short stage races (usually a week in length), and grand tours (stage races three weeks in length). The races are mixed throughout the season, owing largely to tradition, though the schedule has been tweaked in recent years to give the most important races showcase times with minimal conflicts.

The Tour de France is a grand tour, a position it occupies with the other two three-week stage races: Italy's Giro d'Italia, which runs in late May, and Spain's Vuelta a España, which is in September. They also share prestige with the classics, which start in March and are on the calendar until October.

Professional bike racers typically compete in some 50 to 150 races in a season. How many depends on who they are and what's expected of them. Neo-pros are generally given a light load so they can start to adjust to the rigors of racing. Team leaders have some latitude in picking their races; they're allowed to use many races for training so long as they're in peak condition and ready to win their major objectives. Everyone else is told what to race and how to race by the *directeur sportif*. *Domestiques* might have some goal races, too, but even when they're given a schedule at the start of the year, they can expect it to change depending on how they're riding, and where they're needed. Generally, *domestiques* are expected to play a support role, but if they're given a chance to win, they take it—not only for the prize money, but for the points and prestige and the chance to move to a better position on the team or on another team.

It is rare to find a race where every rider is in peak condition. In every race, some of the riders are there for training, even if that training means riding all-out for their team leader. Even with the Tour, there are some riders who are only there to work on their fitness for the major August races. The adage "racing is the best training" is lived by those who go to the Tour looking to build fitness for later races.

And the pros also compete in open races against amateurs when they feel a need to race and there are no races on the pro calendar. While many competitors dislike seeing the best in the sport show up at a local event, it's good for the fans, and the smaller fish often give the big pros a relatively wide berth, on the fear that they'd be the ones responsible for ending a top professional's season.

Training

Training is a twelve-month occupation. The best pros are probably riding 20,000 miles every year. Even when they're in the off-season, they're preparing for the next year. Their idea of a break is two weeks, maybe three, off the bike. And they're probably exercising nearly every day within that time span.

At one time, pros could take it a bit easier. Longer time off the bike, start the season with "easy" races, and then build. But, as there are UCI points on the line at most decent-sized races, and some of the competition is always at peak form, it's hard to take any race easy. Gaining ten pounds—something not hard to do when one is used to gobbling down huge quantities of food to fuel the fire and take on five hundred miles a week—might have been normal at one time, but now racers are watching their weight all the time.

There is a rhythm to training; there are periods of high intensity mixed in with times of low and middle intensity. These rhythms play out day-to-day, week-to-week, and month-to-month. Some days are for riding easy, some for riding at race pace. Teams organize training camps at the start of the season to make sure their riders are training hard. The unspoken rule at training camps is that no one wants to look bad in front of team management. As a result, camps often become grueling affairs where each rider tries to wear down the others. Some teams have smaller groups travel to ride race routes as part of their training as well, and simulating racing on the courses is considered excellent preparation.

What is rarely mentioned about training is that an essential element to training hard is resting hard. If they're riding six hours a day, you can be sure they're not doing anything strenuous for the rest of their waking hours. It's more like eating, sitting around, getting a massage, and sleeping as much as possible. An afternoon nap between eating after training and dinner is not uncommon. An ad featuring Belgian star Tom Boonen showed him lying on a mattress (one of his team's sponsors makes the mattress), and a caption reading "Tom Trains Day and Night."

Down, but Rarely Out

As with any sport, injuries are expected. Crashing into another rider, a car, a fence, a hold in the road, not simply falling, is the cause of most injuries. And even though most racers expect to go down, the expected result is raw skin, commonly called "road rash," and bruises. Take a look at the pivots (knees, elbows, shoulders, hips, and ankles) on long-time racers and you'll see a subtle patchwork of scars. Road rash and bruising are painful, but rarely enough to drop out of a major race.

Broken bones are rare. The common explanation is that pros know how to react to crashing because they've practiced tumbling, but it's just as likely that they don't stiffen their bodies as they go down. The most common break is the collarbone. It doesn't take a tremendous amount of force to break, but thankfully most fractures heal pretty quickly. And even when fractures take a while to heal, the racers are doing what they can to stay in shape, or lose as little fitness as possible. As soon as they can, they're back on the bike, riding.

Despite the obvious dangers associated with racing, most cyclists will tell you that training is more dangerous. Even car racers have discussed how driving outside of racing is more dangerous. Pro racers are training on open roads, during all weather conditions. It's the distracted, non-professional drivers that add the danger.

Helmet Hatred

Take a look at older pictures of the Tour, and you'll certainly notice that few racers wore helmets. Until recently, helmet use has been optional in the pro ranks. In terms of technology, helmets that actually protected one's head have only been around since 1975, and lightweight versions have only been in existence since 1986. As helmet technology improved, racers started wearing them more often.

Those who don't like racing in helmets point to the safety of the closed course and being surrounded by professionals, note that there are very few head injuries among cyclists, that even among the few pro cyclists who have died from head injuries, some were wearing hard-shell helmets, and ultimately, since it is their livelihood, they should be trusted to make a wise judgement on the matter.

Those who don't like wearing helmets seem to think of them as an encumbrance, a discomfort, something that adversely affects their performance. Many find them distractingly uncomfortable on hot days, particularly, when climbing. This is why many cyclists are bare-headed during mountain stages.

Interestingly, many fans and photographers prefer bare-headed riders. The helmetless rider is easier to individuate, easier to see as human, and shows more expression. Facial expressions are a reason race photographers also lamented the acceptance of sunglasses amongst racers.

Drugs

Sports have been increasingly linked to illegal, performance-enhancing drugs. And the pro cycling world in general, and the Tour in particular, has had its share of scandals and high-profile busts. The positive drug tests indicate that some people are taking advantage of the dark side to do well.

Arguably, cycling is doing more about stopping the cheats than other sports. It's a rarely remarked irony that the more pro cycling does to root out doping, the more people are caught, which then gives cycling a "dirty" reputation, while the efforts should mean cycling is cleaner than the sports that do less to catch dopers. Until high-profile positive drug tests rocked the sport in 2005, Major League Baseball had a fairly lax antidrug policy in comparison to cycling. Before then, the policy was a ten-game suspension for a positive drug test, and little mention of amphetamine usage. After the 2005 scandals, MLB decided they needed tougher penalties. For 2006, a positive drug test will result in a fifty-game suspension, a second positive, a one-hundred game suspension, a third positive, a lifetime ban. They also added a twenty-five-game suspension for getting caught with amphetamines. And, as with fans of American pro sports, it seems like many cycling fans aren't as interested in rooting out the dopers as they are with seeing a great race.

One difference with European cycling is that European governments take the usage of illegal drugs more seriously than non-European governments. The police are getting involved in Europe under the guise of preventing "sporting fraud." Cycling is also working with the World Anti-Doping Agency (WADA) to test all racers and punish those caught. Is cycling doing enough? Hard to say. If negative tests are a good sign, then cycling is doing all right.

Drugs were first reported being used by pro cyclists as early as the 1920s. It came out of the "Forcats de la Route" story by Albert Londres. The response wasn't so much shock at the use, but outrage at the inhuman expectations of race promoters that forced cyclists to take the drugs.

Drug use became less acceptable as time went on. In 1966, dope testing started. But the death of Tom Simpson on Mont Ventoux during the 1967 Tour de France might have convinced many of the importance of eliminating illegal drugs. Simpson collapsed on a blazing hot day within a kilometer of the summit finish. His last words were, "Put me back on my bike," which the fans did, and he rode on a few meters more, collapsed again, and died. Simpson had taken a dangerous mix of amphetamines and alcohol on an infernally hot day.

The next big flare-up with drugs for the Tour was in 1998. Some dubbed it the Tour of Shame. The blame was largely on the Festina team, which was caught with illegal performance-enhancing drugs and thrown out of the Tour. The Festina scandal focused attention on the sport's drug use not only from the UCI but also European police forces, as a French border patrol found the drugs in the trunk of a team car. A second team dropped out of the race to protest being searched. A third dropped out in sympathy with the ousted riders. Since then, both testing and police searching have not only become more common but more stringent.

Every year, several pro cyclists get caught doping. There are in-competition tests where the victor and some random racers are tested. There are surprise tests performed on teams during stage races where the entire team is woken up early and tested. There are also surprise out-of-competition tests performed on riders wherever they live. Rarely does a racer test positive at the Tour, as there are plenty of screening tests during the year and immediately preceding the race, both in and out of competition. Someone who tests positive at his pre-Tour physical isn't allowed to start the race. Occasionally, it's a big name who gets caught, but knowing that a victory guarantees a drug test might deter those who know they'll test positive. Tour champion Marco Pantani was busted while leading the Giro d'Italia several years ago. Even though he came back, the experience changed him and he committed suicide via cocaine overdose in 2004.

The unfortunate thing about the presence of drugs in sport is that anyone who does well can easily be accused of doping. Why is someone doing well? Detractors will often point to drug use. It's an easy explanation for how someone was able to improve.

Lance Armstrong is the rare cyclist who can admit to using a performance-enhancing drug out of competition. It should be noted that Armstrong claims to have given money to UCI to increase drug testing. The drug EPO is a blood-thickening agent used to help cancer victims survive chemotherapy, which is how Armstrong got it and used it when survival was his main concern. It's also a banned performance-enhancing drug, blamed for the death of several cyclists. When Armstrong returned to top form and rode better than ever, there were whispers of drug use. The price of being the most famous cyclist in the world is a bulls-eye on the back, and skeptics and naysayers naturally pored over every aspect of Armstrong's life. Nothing has been proven though there have been allegations by former teammates, employees, and associates. In the fall of 2005, there were stories that Armstrong's blood samples saved from the 1999 Tour tested positive with a new drug test. Since the test in question didn't follow proper protocol, the result is inadmissible. Since it is inadmissible, Armstrong can neither be penalized, nor can he claim damage. In this respect, the result was neither a positive nor a negative test.

Death in the *Peloton*

Yes, people have died bike racing, though not often—and rarely is it because of the racing itself. More often it's because a car gets in the middle of a race when it shouldn't be there and an unlucky racer is in the wrong place at the wrong time.

There have been a few high-profile deaths that have shaken the sport. In 2003, Kazakh racer Andrei Kivilev was racing the Paris-Nice stage race when he had a freak crash. He hit his helmetless head on the ground and immediately went into a coma. He died shortly thereafter. This death triggered a move to make helmet use mandatory in the pro ranks, something pros had been fighting against since 1990. Eight years earlier, in 1995, Italian Fabio Casartelli, also helmetless, crashed and hit his head on a descent in the Tour. The first death in the Tour occurred in 1935 when Francesco Cepeda crashed descending the Col du Galibier.

Paris and Beyond

Lore has it that the Tour changes people, both as people and as bike racers. Many believe that even if a racer suffers through the Tour to finish as the *lanterne rouge*, the fitness gained and tolerance for pain learned will do him in great stead. In terms of changing bodies, the effort expended to finish the Tour usually means one's body weight drops, body fat disappears, and even bone matter atrophies. While a night of partying in Paris is the way most racers celebrate, they're back on their bikes in a few days, and back to the routine of racing and training, training and racing.

Some of the stars will sign contracts to ride exhibition races immediately after the Tour. This has become a little less common recently—riders earn more money now, so they aren't always looking to boost their income. But the pro racing schedule resumes the weekend after the Tour finishes, so there are important races that can't be missed.

Of course they're tired, but riders will tell you cycling is also a job and it beats working. Just as any pro athlete would say.

5

THE ROUTE

Bike racers love to say that the racers make the race. Just like in poker, it isn't so much the cards but the competition that influences how you play the game. The Tour organizers beg to differ, and they change the course every year, just to make this point. The route certainly can influence the outcome, and the route chosen does affect the race. It's so important that those who consider themselves race favorites make a point of attending the presentation where the next year's Tour route is unveiled, and the contenders for the overall scout out what they consider the pivotal stages in training.

Setting the Course

When the Tour first started, such a race was uncharted territory and Desgrange could do as he pleased. Now that there are more than a hundred years of history behind the Tour, a full calendar of cycling events, and concern for the riders' health, there are limits to what the Tour can do. The Union Cycliste International (UCI) bylaws state that a Major Tour (the Tour de France is one of three) can be fifteen to twenty-three days in total length, with stages averaging no more than 180 km (112.5 miles) a day, the longest stage being no longer than 260 km (162.5 miles). Individual and team time trials can be no longer than 80 km each (50 miles). The prologue time trial can be no longer than 8 km (5 miles). The total distance of the Tour can be no longer than 3,500 km (2,187.5 miles). There also must be two rest days.

In addition to the UCI rules, there is a basic structure the Tour usually follows, but after that, the route is up for grabs. Amaury Sport Organization (ASO) decides the route based on a number of factors, including tradition, history, competition, commerce, television, novelty, and balance. And within those factors, they have wide sway.

As the Tour developed, the promoters tried new things, initially to make the race harder, but then to make it more interesting. Stages were shortened, and the number of stages was increased. Mountains were first added in 1905; high mountains in 1910. The Tour first visited a foreign country in 1906. After years of following a clockwise route around France, the Tour first tried a counterclockwise route in 1913. When the Tour started in Evian in 1926, it was the first time the race started outside of Paris. The first team time trial occurred a year later. 1934 brought the first individual time trial. 1939 was the inauguration of the uphill time trial. The first mountaintop finish was added in 1952. The first start outside of France was in 1954, when the race started in Amsterdam. The prologue time trial was added in 1967. The Tour first finished on the Champs Elysées in 1975.

Most of these elements have remained in the Tour—in some form—since their inception. The route traditionally alternates between racing clockwise and counterclockwise around France. On the clockwise years, the Alps are ridden first, on the counterclockwise, the Pyrenees. On alternating years, mostly, the Tour visits a foreign country as part of the route.

The race almost always starts with a prologue of a few kilometers, though occasionally, it's either a much longer time trial or a team time trial. The race almost always has a team time trial in the first week, and one (usually two, occasionally three time trials) for the rest of the race. The last time trial occurs a day or two before the finish in Paris. There is usually a train transfer from the penultimate stage to suburban Paris for the final stage. Every few years, one of the time trials is a climb up a mountain. While the prologue is never more than eight kilometers, the distances of the other time trials are always tinkered with.

There are usually flat stages in the opening week, before the first mountain range is reached. Flat stages traditionally don't reappear until the final week, after the final mountain range. Occasionally, the organizers will route the race over some old cobblestone roads to add drama to the flat stages. The cobbles can present a major obstacle to the racers. Occasionally, a stage will take in part of a "classic" bike racing route, like when it races through Roubaix in the north or the Ardennes region of Belgium.

For the stage or stages between the Alps and Pyrenees, the terrain is usually rolling. Occasionally, the days will be flat. Once in a while, there will be no "easy" days between the two ranges, and the stages are constructed to make it seem as if the Alps and Pyrenees are one massive mountain range.

The mountain stages vary between those with summit finishes and those with town finishes. Town finishes mean the racers zoom off a mountain in the final kilometers of a race, and the long descent often results in close finishes where the climbers first take an advantage over the summit of a climb, and those dropped by the summit race at the edge of control to get back in contention before the finish. Summit finishes are grueling and slow, with no room for the riders to recover once on edge.

The last stage has always finished in Paris. For years, the race rode to the Parc des Princes Velodrome, and riders sprinted for the finish on the track in front of a packed stadium. The velodrome no longer exists, but the current race is too big and fast to make this kind of finish safe. After the velodrome, promoters then tried making the final day a time trial into Paris. Finally, in 1975, they decided on a circuit race around the Champs-Elysées (Elysian Fields), where the race has finished ever since. Only once have they planned a time trial on the Champs for the final day. The Champs finish is a great metaphor, bringing the racers to heaven—not bad after three weeks of hell.

"Tweaking" the Course

The point of having all these elements is that the designers can tweak them to keep the race interesting. Part of the reasoning for this is to keep the race close. The hope is that the race will, over the course of three weeks, develop into a battle between the time trial specialists and the climbers. Early on, the sprinters and opportunists will also have their days, virtually guaranteeing that the lead will change several times. And the route changes often dictate modification in tactics. Teams tweak their Tour lineup before the race depending not only on who's riding well, but who is better at riding the kind of terrain the Tour encompasses that year.

When the Tour seems to be dominated by a particular kind of racer one year, the organizers tweak the course so it will be a bit different the next. If it seems like time trial specialists dominated one year, mountains are added and time trial stages are shortened. If someone wins with a weak team, then the team trial stage could be lengthened.

Unfortunately, or fortunately, the greatest champions have a habit of finding a way to adapt to the changes thrown at them and win despite having a course that doesn't seem suited to their strengths. Armstrong, like Hinault, Merckx, LeMond, and Fignon in their prime, seemed to be able to both "out-climb" the climbers and "out–time trial" the time trialists. A climber like Pantani won in the mountains and limited his losses in the time trials. A *roleur* (a good time trialist) like Induráin found his winning margin in the Race of Truth (time trial) and then hung on to the climbers, limiting his losses in the mountains. Ullrich, always an impressive time trialist, won his Tour by first winning in the mountains, then found the mountains wore him down.

The Tour also likes to honor history. It will honor itself by visiting past glories on anniversaries, and will honor the region in the same way. For the one hundredth anniversary of the Tour, the race started in Paris and had stage finishes in all six of the original host cities. To mark the two hundredth anniversary of the French Revolution, the final stage was a time trial from Versailles to Paris. To celebrate the creation of the European Union, the 1992 Tour visited Spain, Belgium, Holland, Germany, and Italy. The Tour used the Chunnel in 1994 to visit Britain for two stages.

The race used to finish on July 14th, Bastille Day. Finishing in Paris on Bastille Day had great resonance, but the demands of the racing calendar, and probably the French civic calendar as well, had an effect on the Tour. Today, the Tour generally starts the first Saturday in July, though it has been moved around in years to minimize conflict with soccer's World Cup and the Olympics, the only two sporting events that are possibly bigger than the Tour on an international level.

And novelty does have its part in planning the route.

The 1987 Tour started in West Berlin, Germany—the first and only time the race started behind the Iron Curtain of Cold War Europe. Fittingly, a Polish rider, Lech Piasecki, took the yellow jersey on the second stage in Berlin. Every few years, Tour officials seem to look for a new place to start the race, like Montreal, Martinique, or New York (the logistics of getting everyone across the Atlantic and back have prevented this spectacle from being a serious consideration). And they also look for roads and obstacles that haven't been raced on before, or infrequently used. Every so often, the race finishes a stage at Mont Saint Michel, a medieval fortress where the road is submerged by the tide part of every day. It's also a major tourist attraction.

Commerce is another essential element to the creation of the Tour route. Towns pay to host the start and finish of the stages. At first it might seem like towns are buying a white elephant at auction. Imagine paying for the right to have thousands of people descend on your town and party there—and to do so, you need to not only repave roads and redesign major traffic arteries, but have local businesses close up shop. But there is logic to paying. Hosting the Tour is wonderful "free" advertising; it is also a major boost for tourism. Images of the town will be shown worldwide, and the town's name will be in newspapers everywhere. The mayor starts the race that departs from his town, and the mayor of the finish town greets the race leader on the podium. And all those people descending on the town have to stay somewhere, and they have to eat. Besides, having a stage start or finish in a town is a great way to celebrate a local anniversary.

The first summit stage finish, at l'Alpe d'Huez in 1952, came about through commerce. The ski resort had just been built, and the hoteliers wanted to put their name on the map. It is now one of the most famous climbs in cycling. Likewise, other ski resorts have hosted stage finishes to increase notoriety. Spa towns, including the

Belgian town of Spa, and other tourist destinations, also pay for the Tour to visit. The interest from the resorts goes both ways, as the Tour benefits from vacationers looking for an activity. They are some of those who line the streets watching the race come by. Likewise, theme parks have paid for the prestige of a Tour stage. Euro-Disney and Futuroscope have hosted stages. So, too, have auto racetracks.

The search for host towns and the money they bring into the race caused a development known as split stages, which is when more than one stage is run on a single day. To visit more towns and rake in more cash, the Tour organizers started split stages in 1934, with up to three short stages in a single day. The concept was popular with the promoters, but it was equally unpopular with the riders. Even if the money was good, split stages were felt to make racing too hard. The practice largely ended in 1978 when rising star Bernard Hinault led a racer protest against the practice, though for many years after race officials scheduled the occasional split stage, often on the day of the team time trial, through 1987.

Television coverage of the Tour does a great job of advertising France—the race is shown on public television stations in France, so the government is a partner in the development and promotion. Television revenue, garnered from selling rights to television markets around the world, has become the biggest single source of income for the Tour. And with television so important, the needs of producers have been addressed. In a certain sense, this preoccupation is just a continuation of the days of Desgrange and *L'Auto*; Desgrange tried to arrange the finish times so that other papers couldn't scoop him. He was skeptical that other media could help his event, as he believed it would only hurt *L'Auto* circulation.

Goddet, and subsequent Tour directors, took an opposite tack. They decided to embrace developments in media. Today, the stages are run at times when live television will have high viewership, and many of the important stages come on the weekend. Visuals are important for television, so having picturesque villages to race through and stunning backdrops is important. The beautiful locations—gotta have the helicopter cameras out!—sell France as a tourist destination not only to the French, but to the world.

The Tour can go over as many or as few mountains as ASO wants. But ASO generally tries to vary them year to year. Even if they want a savage race, they don't need to route the course over all of the most savage climbs. It is said that there are twenty major mountain climbs in France. These are huge ascents that climb forever and go over high mountains, which will affect the outcome of the race. Most people who follow the race can probably name a good portion of them: Col du Tourmalet, Col de Galibier, l'Alpe d'Huez, Mont Ventoux, among others. Every year, about half of them are used in the Tour. It isn't only that they're climbed during the race, but when they're climbed in the stage and what comes both before and after that matters. Ventoux usually hosts the finish of a stage, but occasionally the finish is in the valley after the climb. When the finish is at the summit, the stage is always won by a climber, while the valley finish has long favored breakaway riders who aren't stellar climbers.

Closing the Road

Since the Tour is such a highly sought-after event, and an advertisement for all of France, ASO has a fair amount of leverage when asking for changes in roads. It isn't uncommon for roads to be repaved and traffic circles changed based on a request by ASO. Most municipalities think a Tour visit is worth the expense of fixing things up. The Tour usually makes a great excuse for holding a party in the town to celebrate when the race comes by.

One of the big things about the Tour is that the race

virtually owns the roads they travel upon. Starting at least two hours before the stage passes on a particular spot, the roads are closed. In the mountains, a pass can be closed all day. Once the roads are closed, it is impossible to move on that road with a car, though bicycles can often ride through hours before the race passes. First, the Caravane Publicitaire, publicity caravan, goes through. It's a Mardi Gras across France, and all manner of freebies are tossed (more on this in a later chapter). Then there is a gap; then the race passes through.

Preceding the publicity caravan, riding with the publicity caravan, as well as preceding the race, riding with, and following the race is a squadron of *gendarmes* (French police) on motorcycles. They help create a rolling enclosure by making sure every intersection is blocked off, directing racers, and corralling every errant vehicle that might pose a threat to the race.

After the race, the roads are still closed until the *voiture balai*, or broom wagon, passes. The broom wagon literally sweeps the course. It picks up the racers too tired or injured to pedal at a speed that will allow them to finish within the time limit. For years, there was a broom affixed to the van, though these days it is not present.

Ritual of the Route

Every day of the Tour starts at the *Ville Depart*, or starting village. It's a traveling village that fits within the actual village hosting the race. Most likely, the racers already had breakfast, but they can snack, get their hair cut, call home, get coffee, read the newspapers, and check their e-mail at the *Ville Depart* every morning. Booths are sponsored, and often teams in the race have celebrities and bigwigs on hand to mix with those who have some connection to the race. Meanwhile, there are also activities for the public outside the area closed for the race. Part of the day's starting is that the racers have to physically sign in before starting the stage. There is an announcer present to call out the racers as they sign in. He makes every racer, no matter how unknown, seem like a star. In between announcing the racers, there's both a magician and stunt bicycle rider present to entertain the crowd with tricks. This is also the time for gladhanders and autograph-seekers to do their thing while enjoying croissants and coffee provided by race sponsors.

Every bike racer knows it's a good idea to get to the start early. Aiming to arrive at the start two hours early is not uncommon, just in case cars get lost, break down, get stuck in traffic, etc. And once there, it's a good idea to make a final check of everything just to be safe. Sometimes, if the hotel is close enough, racers will ride to the start.

Tour stages generally start around noon—earlier for the longer stages and later for the shorter ones. The races typically finish around five in the afternoon. Part of the reasoning certainly has to do with scheduling for television. Even if the stage runs behind schedule, one can interview the stage winner, the protagonists, and the race leaders, and still have it all together for the evening news.

Rollout

When it is time to get the race underway, the racers line up. First there are announcements, bringing up local officials noting important things, for both the racers and the gathered spectators. Then the racers are called up, particularly those leading various competitions and other noteworthy competitors.

When the racers get the signal and roll off, the race hasn't actually begun. In most cases, the first several kilometers are a parade of sorts, where the race is neutralized until the outskirts of town. Many times the roads are pretty narrow and hard for racing, and since the stages are plenty long, the rollout gives the racers a chance to warm up a bit. And it is certainly a plus that the assembled spectators will have an easy time recognizing their favorite racers. Once the edge of town is reached, there's an official with a flag marking where the race actually begins.

Kilometer Zero

The race begins at what is known as kilometer zero. It's hard to know ahead of time if the race will start fast or slow, though having an intermediate sprint or king of the mountain (KoM) sprint early in the stage often means the pace will be hard, as people are looking for those points.

There are also signs placed along the road indicating how far not only to the finish, but to the sprint lines. The signs aren't every kilometer, but at regular enough intervals that the signs do help the racers figure out how far there is to go—an extra reminder on top of the cyclometer most bikes sport, a miniature map of the stage many carry in their pocket, and the radio communication most have with their director.

Finish Lines en Route

Both intermediate sprints and KoMs constitute races within the race, as there are finish lines in towns and atop hills along the course. Intermediate sprints occur two to three times a stage. Generally, there are three sprints on the flatter stages and two on the hilly stages. At the very least, it forces the racers to race for these prizes, as there is the green jersey, money, and publicity attached to the competition. It also works for the towns that are hosting the sprints, as they can draw a crowd to watch the race come through at full steam.

The KoM is basically an uphill intermediate sprint. There are categorized and uncategorized climbs in the Tour. The uncategorized are considered too short and easy to be worthy of mention, though racers all say stages in the Tour are much hillier than advertised by the organizers. There are five categories of hills in the Tour, from short pimples to brutal mountain passes. At the top of each categorized climb, there is a finish line, and the first people over, as with the intermediate sprints, win both points and money, and are in pursuit of the climber's polka-dot jersey.

Also along the route are feed zones. As you can imagine, racers burn through a prodigious amount of calories every day. They start with two bottles of liquid on their bikes and pockets full of food, but that isn't enough to sustain them for the 160 km average stage distance. Since the racers must eat enough to finish, there is at least one feed zone on every stage. The longest stages have two feed zones.

Feed Zones

The feed zone is the officially-mandated place to pick up sustenance. Every team sends a few *soigneurs* to staff it. The *soigneurs* pack musette bags that each rider will pick up as they race by. The musette is just big enough to fit a few bottles as well as energy bars, bananas, sandwiches, etc.

Everyone needs these feeds, so there is some etiquette involved in riding through the zones. The big thing is not to attack in the feed zone. Everyone needs to eat, and forcing a racer off his meal can have consequences down the road.

But having the feeds isn't enough on hot days. Team

cars have an ample supply of drinks that riders can go back and get, though it's usually a *domestique* fetching water for the leader—the energy of the leader must always be conserved. It's not uncommon to see a *domestique* carrying six or more bottles in his pockets and stuffed down his jersey as he rides to the front to feed his teammates. And then the race has a feed motorcycle that often zooms through the field, letting riders pick up bottles this way.

Bottles are a popular souvenir for race fans, and an easy one for riders to give. Since few teams want to deal with the hassle of washing each and every bottle, the riders are instructed to toss them away when emptied. No one wants to get sick from a used bottle. Knowing a bottle is popular swag, riders often try to toss them to fans.

Hometown Heroes

It is inevitable that several French and France-based racers will have the route pass by their hometowns over the course of any Tour. In days gone by, it was common for a racer to get permission from the *peloton* to ride ahead, greet his townspeople, and then wait for the Tour to catch up. While this tradition is much less common today, as the stages are more competitive, it still does occur. The town is out in force, partying. The rider pulls up, is the recipient of a toast, maybe a song from the local band, and then has to jump back into the *peloton* as the field rides by.

Neutralizing the Race

No matter how hard the Tour tries to keep the racing safe and unimpeded on the roads, it is inevitable that things will interfere with the race. Often times, it is a road made impassable by events beyond the organizer's control: a bridge gave way, an oil spill, a protest, snow, flooding, etc., call for action on the promoters' part. After a consultation with the commissaire's panel, the race may be stopped temporarily to be started later, stopped for the day, re-routed, or cancelled.

The big deal is what to do if a breakaway was up the road. If the stage is to be continued, the breakaway starts with the same time gap the riders had at the point the race was stopped. This observation and preservation of the time gap is also an essential part of stopping the race at railroad crossings. If the breakaway has less than a thirty-second lead on the *peloton* or if the break doesn't get stopped at the crossing, the race continues on. If the break has more than a thirty-second lead and gets caught at the crossing, then the race is neutralized and restarted with the breakaway being given a head start equal to their time gap. If the field gets caught at the crossing, it is taken as part of the race, and the officials don't take any action.

Flame Rouge

The final kilometer is marked by a red flag, known as the *flame rouge*, the red flame. Nowadays, the flag is attached to an enormous inflated arch, so the marker is impossible to miss. The flag is a good reminder to know when to start launching one's final effort. The flag also meant that if one crashed between the flag and the stage finish, one wouldn't be docked any time for seconds lost due to the mishap. So long as one got up and made his way across the finish line, one could start the next day. The final kilometers are usually the only point in the stage when fencing is put on both sides of the road to keep the spectators away from the racers when the race is in its most frenzied state.

Awards Presentation

After every stage, there is an awards presentation on a stage at or near the finish line. It often starts as the final stragglers are crossing in to the finish line. Podium girls help present prizes to the stage winner and the holders of the various jerseys. Local dignitaries are also on the stage to greet the riders.

And when the day is done, the riders talk about who or which team made the race happen, while the promoters are inevitably discussing how the course helped frame the outcome.

6

THE JERSEYS

All teams in sports and in most walks of life want a distinct identity to separate themselves from the pack. Home and away uniforms are common in American team sports, and many teams have clothes for special occasions or to honor their past history.

Cycling is no different. Each team of nine riders in the Tour is expected to wear identical clothing, with a few exceptions. At one time, taste and technology limited the design options—black shorts, white socks, wool jerseys of a few different colors, at most. Embroidery of sponsor names on the jersey or shorts was an advance. But, as rules and tastes changed and technology improved, it has become possible to come up with clothes as crazy or as staid as anyone can imagine.

Nowadays, team clothing is generally plastered with sponsor names. The socks, shorts, gloves, jerseys, hats, and helmets are all designed together so no matter how you view a rider, you know what he's riding and whom he rides for. Often shoes and glasses are color-coordinated along with the bicycle, handlebar tape, and saddle. The distinctive ensembles are good for spectators, who have an easier time picking out riders and knowing their affiliations when the clothing is markedly different than anything else out there.

It took a few years after the Tour started for practical race clothing to be determined. The first winner was known for riding in a white jacket, and most cyclists rode in knickers, but this getup was probably neither practical nor comfortable. Quickly, racers turned to wool jerseys and shorts, often accompanied by a cap and goggles, too. And after a day on the road, most were encased in road grime. And because of the nature of the times, they probably washed their clothes out in a sink and wore the same clothes for the next stage—some racers are still doing this today, though not at the Tour.

The Origins of the Yellow Jersey
(Maillot Jaune)

The idea of a yellow jersey to separate the race leader from the rest of the pack did not originate with the first Tour de France. When it appeared, it was an ingenious development. Not only does the Tour still employ a leader's jersey, but so does just about every stage race in the world and most race series. Thanks to the Tour, yellow is almost always the color of the leader's jersey around the world.

There are two stories about when the jersey originated. In both stories, the point of the distinctive jersey is to make it easy for spectators to know who the leader is. The first theory is that Belgian Philippe Thys wore the first yellow jersey in 1913 as race leader. Thys claims it was suggested by Desgrange and urged by his bike sponsor, Peugeot. Thys is the only source for this story, and the Tour's official history differs.

The Tour claims the first yellow jersey was awarded on stage 10 of the 1919 Tour. There are a number of theories as to how the leader's jersey got its color. The popular explanation is yellow was chosen because *L'Auto* was printed on yellow paper. And people point to the Giro d'Italia, where the leader's jersey is pink, the same color of the pages of *La Gazzetta dello Sport*, that race's sponsor. There is some debate as to the validity of this theory. Others suggest a yellow jersey was the only jersey found when they looked for a jersey to present the race leader. Another theory still is that yellow wool was the only jersey material available because of a postwar wool shortage. That Desgrange was famously thrifty helps convince some of the latter theories.

Whatever the reason, the jersey was a success. More people noticed who the leader was as the racers passed by on the road, and the riders could tell who it was when they were racing—which was a disadvantage to the leader, and a boon to the challengers.

Today, the organizers are firm in their conviction that the yellow jersey must stand out; they do not allow anyone else to wear yellow jerseys during the race. If yellow is the main color of a Tour team's jersey, they have to come up with an alternate color scheme for the duration of the Tour. In the 1980s, the Kas team normally wore a yellow jersey with blue accents; for the Tour, they changed to blue jerseys with yellow accents. In the 1990s, the ONCE team wore yellow jerseys for most of the year and switched the main color to pink for the duration of the Tour. In 2000, The Mercatone Uno team switched from their all-yellow ensemble to an all-pink ensemble, a nice touch considering the leader was Marco Pantani, who had won both the Giro and Tour in the same year.

Wearing yellow, even for one day, is enough to make any racing career a huge success. Forever, any rider who wears the *maillot jaune* is known as a "former holder of the yellow jersey," making it easier to get contracts for riding, for promotional appearances, even for getting announced at races.

Occasionally, racing etiquette prevents the race leader from wearing yellow. If the leader of the race crashes out one day, it is common that the person who has inherited the race lead forgoes wearing the jersey the next day. This is both to honor the fallen rider and to say that luck is not a way to earn the most coveted prize in cycling.

The defending champion starts the prologue last and is expected to race the short test in yellow. Armstrong has given a new wrinkle to the honor of yellow by sometimes refusing to wear the yellow skinsuit because he doesn't feel he has earned it; after all, everyone starts from zero.

Polka-Dot Jersey

(Maillot Blanc et Poi Rouge, Maillot Grimpeur)

While the king of the mountain (KoM) competition began in 1933, the KoM jersey did not appear until 1975. The competition was designed to give something to the climbers, an attempt to make up for the time bonuses given for stage wins, which almost always occurred on flat roads in the middle of towns or cities. Points are gained by being among the first people to climb past a finish line atop a hill or mountain.

Every hill beyond a certain length and distance gets a category designation. They're ranked from category four through one, and Hors Category (hc, beyond categorization). The easy ones are category four, and it gets harder from there. The lowest category climb gets the fewest points for winning at the summit, while the highest gets the most. As a result, the most important climbs are at the peaks of the highest mountains. And the points go deeper, the bigger the hill. An easy climb has only three places up for grabs and a few points for each place. The big climbs have the following requirements and point breakdowns, though the last climb of the day carries double points.

CATEGORY 4: 3 km long or less, usually just a slight hill
points: 1. 5, 2. 3, 3. 1

CATEGORY 3: 5 km long or less, a bit steeper than 4 percent
points: 1. 4, 2. 3, 3. 2, 4. 1.

CATEGORY 2: 5–10 km long, steeper than 4 percent
points 1. 10, 2. 9, 3. 8, 4. 7, 5. 6, 6. 5

CATEGORY 1: 10–20 km long, steeper than 5 percent
points: 1. 15, 2. 13, 3. 11, 4. 9, 5. 8, 6. 7, 7. 6, 8. 5

HORS CATEGORY: often 15–20 km long, sections steeper than 10 percent
points: 1. 40, 2. 36, 3. 32, 4. 28, 5. 24, 6. 20, 7. 16, 8. 14, 9. 12, 10. 10

The KoM jersey itself was a product of race sponsorship. Poulain Chocolates was the sponsor of the competition in 1975, and the jersey is a reflection of the wrapper design they employed. Over the years, it has been modified slightly for various sponsors, but it is basically a white jersey with big, red polka dots.

While the top racers for the overall usually gain enough points to be contenders in the KoM competition, a person focusing on the prize generally wins. The contenders don't want to waste energy sprinting to the top of every big mountain, fearing that energy spent will cost them on the final climb of a stage. Riders going for the KoM start competing for the prize pretty much on the first categorized hill, which usually appears on the first stage. Still, there's a difference between winning a small hill and a big mountain, and the lead is often held by a rider who both sprints and climbs decently until the first mountain range is reached. Usually, the lead switches to a specialist at climbing big mountains about halfway through the Tour.

The competition itself doesn't always favor the "pure" climbers, the little riders known as mountain goats who seem to hop uphill easily. Often times, it is the aggressive rider who can climb decently and sprint well who wins the jersey. One year, there was a category-four climb in the prologue, and then not another ranked climb for a few days. Sprinter Marcel Wüst made a point of being the fastest guy up the hill, won the climb, and thus the Tour was treated to the rare sight of seeing the mountains leader mix it up in field sprints for a number of days, even winning field sprint stage victory in the polka dots.

Since the start of the twenty-first century, the strategy for taking the climber's jersey has varied. When he first vied for the title in the 1990s, Frenchman Richard Virenque was a specialist climber. As he developed as a stage racer, he was able to win both the polka dots and compete for the yellow jersey; in 1997, he won the jersey and was second overall. As he got older, he saw his abilities as a climber decline, so he started going on long attacks early in the mountain stages; the moves were almost guaranteed to fail, but so long as he won most of the climbs on the days he went on the attack, he earned the necessary points to gain and secure the lead in the competition.

Virenque's strategy of going on long attacks is one that fellow Frenchman Laurent Jalabert initiated. Jalabert, twice a green jersey winner in the early 1990s, had morphed into a contender for yellow. He decided in the twilight of his career the way to win the *maillot pois* was to live for long attacks. He'd attack early on mountain stages, win the first two or three climbs, and then get caught on the final climb.

As a result of this new strategy, Tour organizers

tweaked the points structure again. Points for doing well on the big cols are now weighted toward the latter climbs on the long, multimountain days, so some of the later climbs get double points.

The Green Jersey
(Maillot Vert)

This is also known as the sprinter's jersey, or the regularity jersey. It is awarded to the rider who has accumulated the most points in both intermediate sprints and stage finishes over the course of the race.

The Green Jersey first appeared with the start of the points competition, which debuted in the 1953 Tour. The competition was first known as the Grand Prix Cinquentenaire, honoring the fiftieth anniversary of the first Tour. The reason for green is that a store specializing in garden supplies, Belle Jardinier, was the inaugural sponsor.

The Green Jersey was good for commerce and good for racing. It became the second jersey competition and gave something new to the sprinters as well as keeping things interesting for the fans, particularly on the flat stages and in the middle of long stages. It is probably no coincidence that the competition started just as mountaintop finishes were added to the race. Sprinters are often seen as money men, good for always getting in the prize money, which benefits the entire team. American sprinter Davis Phinney, winner of two stages of the Tour in the 1980s, and winner of over three hundred races in the United States, was known as "The Cash Register" for his ability to ring up victories and prize money.

In terms of the form the sprint competition takes, it's fairly easy to understand. There are two to three intermediate sprints every stage, in addition to points available for finishing well. The intermediate sprints only award three places each, so if a rider doesn't think he can get top three, he doesn't sprint—which both saves energy and makes it safer for the pack.

What gets tricky when scoring the green jersey competition is there are often time bonuses attached to intermediate sprints and finishes.

INTERMEDIATE SPRINTS
1st: 6 points, 2nd: 4, 3rd: 2

FLAT STAGES
35, 26, 24, 22, 20, then down one point at a time to 25th place

ROLLING STAGES
22, 20, 18, 16, 15, then down one point at a time to 20th place

MOUNTAIN STAGES
17, 15, 13, 12, 10, then down one point at a time to 15th place.

TIME TRIALS
15, 12, 10, 8, 6, 5, then down one point at a time to 10th place

Often, there are time bonuses for the top three places as well. A time bonus in stage racing means that one's time is reduced by the amount of the bonus. Generally, the bonuses are six, four, and two seconds for the first three riders across the intermediate sprint or finish line, though finish-line points can be a good bit higher, such as twelve seconds for a victory. Year to year, the time bonus idea is tweaked, but the rules are clear before the race starts. Time bonuses are almost never offered for top finishes in time trials, are usually awarded for finishes on flat stages, and sometimes awarded for top finishes on mountain stages.

The time bonuses usually mean that the yellow and green jerseys are swapped amongst sprinters in the opening week of the race. Occasionally, a rider is leading both the points competition and the overall. He's expected to wear yellow, and the second-place rider in the points competition gets the green. Once in a long while, time bonuses are used to change the final general classification, a tactic Alexandre Vinokourov used in 2005 to steal fifth overall from Levi Leiheimer on the final stage.

Once the Tour enters the mountains, the riders known as "pure sprinters," meaning they can't go uphill well, either drop out of the race or suffer just to hang on, and the sprinters who can climb moderately well gain points by hanging onto the lead group until the first or second intermediate sprint, winning points, then dropping off the lead to save their energy for another day. Since there are flat stages in the last week of the race, and the Champs-Elysées is a popular stage for sprinters, most riders want to stay in the race to make it to the end.

It should also be noted that the Tour organization frowns on riders dropping out of the race merely because it is hard. Super Mario Cipollini, the self-proclaimed king of the sprinters, who dominated bunch sprints from the 1990s into the twenty-first century, had to suffer the humiliation—more likely his sponsor suffered the lack of exposure—of not being invited to the Tour on several occasions because he had a reputation of quitting the race once the mountains got hard. Despite wearing the yellow and green jerseys on a number of occasions and setting the record for consecutive stage victories, he never finished a Tour.

White Jersey
(Maillot Blanc)

The white jersey is awarded for the best young rider competition, the highest placed rider on general classification under the age of twenty-five. Twenty-five might not seem like a young rider to many, but in the cycling world, lore has it, and history has shown, the racers don't enter their peak years until their late twenties. This doesn't mean that the under-twenty-five crowd isn't competitive, only that it's somewhat unusual for them to have the stamina and strength to survive a three-week race in good form. Laurent Fignon and Jan Ullrich won both the Tour and the best young rider competition in 1983 and 1997, respectively. Several others, including Greg LeMond in 1984 and Jan Ullrich in 1996, won the competition and finished on the podium.

This competition was started in 1975, when Italy's Francesco Moser won it while finishing seventh overall. One of the things the white jersey does is identify stars of the future. Moser went on to have a long and successful pro career, winning world competitions, the Giro, a number of classics, and breaking the hour record in 1984. While only two other white jersey winners, Greg LeMond and Marco Pantani, went on to win the Tour, most of the other winners had long careers near the top of the sport. The jersey disappeared after 1989. The white jersey itself reappeared in 2000.

Retired Jerseys—Red, Patchwork

In the 1980s, the Tour added both a red jersey for the leader in the intermediate sprint competition and a "patchwork" jersey for the person doing the best at all the competitions. The patchwork was a bit like having the yellow, green, white, red, and polka-dot jerseys in one jersey. The reason for these competitions was probably both to add money and excitement to the race. The red and patchwork jerseys were dropped after the 1989

Tour, allegedly to simplify things. That year, Irishman Sean Kelly won both the green and red jerseys.

Major Prizes

Red Number Bib The red number bib is a daily award given to the most aggressive rider on a particular stage. Sometimes called "combativity," it is awarded on a points basis by journalists watching the stage. For the next stage, the rider's race number, which he uses throughout the race, usually a black number on a white background, is replaced with a white number on a red background.

The points are awarded every day and tallied at the end of the Tour. The person with the highest points total is awarded a prize for the most aggressive racer. Many might think that the winner of the Tour is the most aggressive. This has yet to be the case, though second-place finisher Laurent Fignon won the award in 1989. The award goes to those who make a habit of going on long breakaways. Most fail, but their attacks animate the race. Jacky Durand, a French rider who rode from the 1990s into the twenty-first century, seemed to like nothing more than attacking at kilometer zero and staying away as long as possible. He was good at it, the crowds seemed to love him for it, and he often won the aggressive rider competition.

Team Classification The team prize is an essential element of the Tour. There is both a daily and overall team prize. For many years, the team leading this competition was awarded yellow cycling caps. The caps were dropped as hard-shell helmets came onto the scene, but the competition still acts the same way. The daily prize is determined by adding up the times of the top three finishers on each team. The overall lead is determined by taking the cumulative of each team's daily team ranking. The leading team is awarded small stuffed lions, the symbol of the competition's sponsor, Credit Lyonnais.

Other Special Jerseys

Rainbow Jersey (Maillot Arc-en-Ciel) Arguably, this is the second-most coveted jersey in cycling. Give it up for those who are so comfortable in their masculinity they desire to wear yellow and rainbow (and pink for leading the Giro)! The rainbow jersey—a white jersey with a band across the chest of blue, red, black, yellow, and green—is not a Tour award; rather, it is awarded by the UCI to the winners of the World Championships in every discipline (one jersey for road racing, another for time trials, etc.). Riders are only allowed to race in the jersey when competing in the discipline they won it in. The jerseys are awarded every year.

At one time, it was common to see someone wearing rainbow competing for the Tour victory. LeMond and Hinault both won Tours while reigning world champions. Armstrong, and before him Eddy Merckx, Stephen Roche, and Joop Zoetemelk, all won the worlds and the Tour, though Merckx and Roche are rare in that they won both in the same year.

Nowadays, with increased specializations in racing and a longer race season, it is less common to even see the rainbow jersey worn at the Tour, let alone by a contender. Currently, the world championships are scheduled for October, shortly after the Vuelta a España, so the people who do well at the worlds often race the Vuelta, and are training during the Tour, either by racing the Tour for training or riding at home.

Pro Tour Leader The Pro Tour is a new league and competition, which debuted in 2005. It's hard to say whether or not the league idea and the attendant competition will last. The idea of the Pro Tour is a season-long competition for the best teams in the biggest races. It is a successor to a cycling World Cup, ended in 2004, which itself was a successor to the Super Prestige competition in the 1980s, all of which were designed to unify the calendar and create a ranking for the best racers on any given year.

The current design of the *maillot* is a white jersey with blue bands on the collar and sleeves. While it's hard to say whether or not the competition leader will race the Tour, the points gained by racing it will have an effect on the outcome of the competition.

Italian Danilo DiLuca won the inaugural Pro Tour by racing well in the Spring Classics, then having an impressive Giro d'Italia, where he finished fourth. He skipped the Tour and had an unimpressive fall season. Already there's a discussion that the Pro Tour's points system favors one-day races over stage races, so expect the competition to be altered a bit over the next several years.

National Champions The winner of his nation's national championship is entitled to wear a jersey honoring that victory for the year following the race. National championship races are generally held in late June, right before the Tour begins. For many riders, not only is it a great honor (resulting both in increased publicity for the rider and team, and a boost in his next year's salary); it is also almost a guarantee that the national champion will ride the Tour.

Canada and the United States are exceptions to this rule. Since the travel across the ocean and accordant rest generally take more than a week, the United States holds its professional championships in early June, and Canada holds its in early July. Most Americans serious about doing well at the Tour don't want to lose training time by coming back to the States, and obviously, any Canadian at the Tour can't also compete at his national championship. It's pretty rare to see a reigning national champion from the Americas riding the Tour, though Fred Rodriguez, George Hincapie, Lance Armstrong, and Ron Kiefel have done it. A reigning national champion from Canada has never ridden the Tour.

Most national championship jerseys are fairly simple. They usually follow a three-color pattern that was in vogue when wool jerseys were standard racing gear. Belgium, France, Italy, Luxembourg, the Netherlands, and several other countries utilize a three-color jersey, with the national colors each taking a third of the space—one color for the shoulders and sleeves, one color in the middle, one at the bottom. Sometimes, it can be confusing, as the Netherlands are red, white, and blue, as is Luxembourg, while France is blue, white, and red. Most other nations, like Australia, Germany, and the United Kingdom use a white jersey with the nation's colors in a band across the middle. The United States employs a "Captain America" design with the chest and shoulders blue with white stars, and the bottom half having vertical red and white stripes.

Some teams go crazy with designing unique stuff for their national champion. Sometimes, the shorts, bike, helmet, and shoes are painted or designed to match. Sometimes, they mate the team design with the national champion colors to create a unique look.

Basic Uniform

The only thing that's important now is that every member of each team wears an identical jersey and shorts uniform. It reads redundant, but in 1997, Mario Cipollini of the Saeco-Cannondale team took to wearing unique shorts each day. They had the sponsor's logo in the right places, but instead of his team shorts, he wore stars and stripes shorts one day to honor his American bike sponsor. When he wore the *maillot jaune*, he wore yellow shorts and rode a yellow bike. The team received a hefty fine for his infractions, but the publicity was well worth it. And, over time, wearing shorts that color-coordinate with the Tour's special jersey became more and more common.

Special Uniforms

The Saeco-Cannondale team was the cutting edge of uniform design. When the Tour visited Ireland, the team had special green-and-white jerseys made up that had "WORLD PEACE" in place of their sponsors' names. Tour officials stopped them from wearing the uniform, but Cannondale had other plans for the jersey. They sold the world peace jersey in retail shops.

The publicity gamble was successful enough that every year Cannondale debuts a special jersey one day in the Tour. One year, they honored Caesar with white and gold jerseys stating "VENI, VIDI, VICI." Another year, they made a plea to recognize how light their bikes are: "LEGALIZE MY CANNONDALE" in prison-garb stripes.

Other teams are getting in the act as well. The U.S. Postal Service team debuted pseudo-retro Postal jerseys with the Postal Service logo from the 1970s on the Champs-Elysées for Lance's fifth victory. They busted out yellow-accented team jerseys, shorts, and a "lone star" helmet design on the Champs after his sixth, and the same with the Discovery Channel Pro Cycling Team clothing in the seventh. In both cases, the clothing made it to stores.

It's hard to know if this idea was inspired by professional sports in the United States or not. This concept of the special jerseys seems to be getting ever more attention from many pro teams whether they be in baseball, basketball, football, or hockey.

The Prizes

Every decent result, every point won in the Tour, is worth money. Professional bike racers draw a salary, but they expect to supplement that salary with prize money. As mentioned before, teams share the spoils, often equally, and usually at the end of the year.

The most recent data available for prize money is from 2005. That year, almost three million Euros were up for grabs at the Tour. The Discovery Channel Pro Cycling Team went home with €545,640. €400,000 was for Armstrong winning the race; the rest came from four stage wins, for Yaroslav Popovych winning the Best Young Rider jersey, for high stage finishes, and doing well on the team, points, and climbing competitions. In contrast, the Euskaltel team won €9,310, the lowest prize total. Each road and time trial stage victory was worth €8,000, while coming in third on a category-one climb was worth €150. Winning the green or polka-dot jerseys was each worth €25,000. Just wearing the *maillot jaune* was worth €350, while one of the other special jerseys for a day was worth €300.

There is a second consideration for all the racers: UCI points. Since there is an international ranking system, every individual and team wants to do well, as the ranking can determine not only salary, or whether or not one rides for a team the next year, but also whether or not a team stays within its division or is dropped down for lack of results. The rankings are updated after every race. The points gained from riding well or winning a race are erased when that race starts the following year. There are more points on the line in the biggest events, and the most points are available at stage races, as one can score both by doing well at stages and doing well overall. When the Tour begins, many of the Tour contenders who did well the previous year see their ranking drop precipitously, as they lost all those points from riding well, and the riders who did well in the Spring Classics, early stage races, and the Giro are at the top. By Tour's end, the rankings will be recalculated, and those who rode well will see their rankings rise.

7

RACE IN MOTION

Everyone starts the prologue as equals on time. By the final finish line on the Champs-Elysées, the time gaps between the champion and the *lanterne rouge* could be five hours. Between the two moments, there is almost no end to the tactical possibilities and strategic gambits. Part of the strategy is dependent on the course, part on the weather, part on the competitors. And there is the x-factor of luck and happenstance.

There was a time when racers could afford to take some of the stages at a somewhat leisurely pace for a while. In Tours of yesteryear, it wasn't uncommon for the race to have unofficial stops to snag water, ice cream, or even a glass of wine if the stage was long and hot and the finish was many, many kilometers away. Those days are over. Now that everyone is generally in better shape, not only is the race more competitive, the differences in ability are smaller. Because both professional bike racing and the Tour have grown, the stakes are higher. Stages are rarely leisurely at any point. Attacks can happen at almost any time, often starting at kilometer zero, and everyone has to be more careful with their efforts.

In days gone by, it wasn't unusual for the contenders for the overall title to try to win stages in the time trials, on the flats, and in the mountains. Part of this was due to a team system where every team had one leader and everyone else supported him. And, part of it was due to a less competitive racing atmosphere. Today, most of those chasing the overall victory don't take chances in the bunch sprints, don't attack on the flats, and have their teammates shield them from the wind until the team has been exhausted.

In some respects, the early Tours were more dramatic because of the less competitive scene. Time gaps were bigger, attacks might have been longer. Maurice Garin won the first Tour by almost three hours. Fausto Coppi won the 1952 Tour by almost a half-hour, a "modern" tour record. Race leaders initiating a solo attack over 100 km from the finish of a stage, as Eddy Merckx did in the 1969 tour, wasn't improbable.

Today, the race is often more subtle. Gaining and losing seconds is now a big deal. Riders have to carefully pick their moments for attacks. Go too early, and they might be exhausted too soon. Go too late and they might not be able to take enough time.

Tactically, racing has gotten more sophisticated as well. Most racers carry two-way radios, and are wired to communicate with their fellow teammates and *directeur sportif*. The DS is not only watching the race unfold from behind, but he has Radio Tour (official race news provided by the promoter) giving him race reports, and he might even be taking small glances at the televised race coverage via a mini television in his car's console. He might also have *soigneurs* and other team workers calling in on cell phones to give updates from the road. He can relay information as it's happening, which makes team strategies all the more dynamic.

Factors to Consider

Teams are advertising vehicles for the sponsors. Success is the easiest way for the advertising to work, but exposure is another way, especially when the team isn't winning. Sometimes, television coverage is enough to prompt a breakaway. If the Tour is going to visit the town where a sponsor is headquartered, expect the sponsor's team to make a huge effort to lead the race into that town. If a sponsor is headquartered by a stage finish, expect the sponsor's team to make winning that stage a major race priority.

Aerodynamics plays a large part in figuring out strategy. Basically, once a bicycle and rider are in motion, the power it takes to move through the wind increases exponentially. At speeds of 12 mph, which is what the leading climbers might be riding on the longest climbs, the "draft" provided by a rider or riders in front is negligible. But pedaling along at 25 mph, the average speed for the entire race, the draft created by riders in front or the hole that the lead rider has to punch, is significant, and the energy saved by sheltering behind another rider is measurable. At 40 mph, the speed of some of the finishing sprints, the draft, and corresponding wall of air, is almost a virtual brick wall. At 62 mph, the speed riders can attain screaming off the highest climbs, it is like a concrete-reinforced wall.

There is plenty of strategy that goes into where to find shelter in the pack. Some like to stay at the back to get the biggest draft, while others are concerned that it is also the easiest place to crash, and also the easiest place to miss the big attacks. Other riders like to stay near the front so they can keep tabs on the action and not get caught behind the inevitable crash. A number of team leaders are always surrounded by their *domestiques*, while others choose their spots based on where a favored rider is.

As a result, many of the strategies have to do with saving energy by drafting as much as possible, and expending energy when people can't draft off others. Riders expecting to do well at the end of the stage or race will be protected from the wind by their teammates for as long as possible.

On a flat road, with no crosswind, few riders will get *dropped* (that is, fall behind the pack), even when the pace is the fastest. So, those dreaming of winning the Tour save their energy for times when the race will be the hardest. Usually, those stages are time trials and mountain stages. But a stage with rough cobblestones, or across a region with strong crosswinds, can end the Tour for an unlucky or ill-prepared favorite.

In 1999, the Passage du Gois was included on a flat stage. Though the road is flat, it is slick because it routinely gets flooded by tidal waters. Add a strong wind, and a few favorites lost any chance of winning because they were caught behind crashes. Six minutes lost because of bad luck or habit. In 2004, there was a "Roubaix" stage, where large sections of rough cobblestones were included. Most of the favorites were prepared, but a few weren't. The unfortunate crashed fighting for position on the roads leading up to the cobblestone sections and saw their hopes of overall victory disappear before the first week was over.

Keep in mind that every team and individual wants to win something at some time during the race. Stage wins, wearing one of the special jerseys, finishing the race at the top of a race-long competition is ideal, but even doing well, like placing in an intermediate sprint or climb, finishing in the top ten on a stage, is preferable to nothing. It's not only getting one's name and sponsor into the news, but it's money. And since everyone on a team shares in the prizes, each rider has a stake in his teammates' success.

The most basic scenario is when the *peloton* is riding together, known as riding *en masse*. When someone or a group of people tries to ride away from the *peloton*, that's a breakaway. These are the two most basic racing scenarios. Once a breakaway gets established, the field is in a position to let the breakaway ride away to the finish, or to try to chase it down, so either another breakaway can go or the entire field can finish together.

On flat roads, a breakaway should be no match for the field. A breakaway rarely has more than twenty riders, and the field usually has over 170. The math is on the field's side.

But there are plenty of times when the field can't or won't chase down the breakaway. With the breakaway-chase scenario, a team that has a rider up the road isn't expected to help with the chase. And if a racer up the road refuses to help the breakaway advance, he's supposed to stay out of the way.

Right away, one should see how the tactical possibilities can change. With twenty-two teams in the bike race, if a majority of the teams have someone in the breakaway, the field, as a collective, might not have the desire to chase the breakaway. And, with certain conditions, like bad weather on narrow roads and winds, it is sometimes hard for the big field to get everyone to put in an effort to chase a breakaway.

And, as in any human endeavor, mood can play a part. If it's a hot day, and riders in the field are feeling tired, many might start thinking, *Let the breakaway go; they'll probably cook themselves in the heat and fall apart anyway.* Conversely, if it's a cold and wet day, everyone might assume that the other riders don't want to race, which may result in everyone riding hard, thinking that the others will give up soon.

There are many strategies employed over the course

of the race, and they are always subject to change. When winning the race is suddenly out of the question, the team chooses a new plan for the remainder of the Tour. When an opportunity presents itself, riders might as well take the initiative and see where it leads.

In addition to the obvious offensive strategies of racing hard at the front, there are also defensive strategies. These often consist of teams allowing riders to break away to force rival teams to chase. If a sprinter is in the hunt for points or time at intermediate sprints, the green jersey holder might try to send a rider up the road in the chance that a breakaway will take the points, thus denying them to the rival. If a team has two riders well-placed in the overall, they might send the dark horse rider up the road to force the yellow jersey and his team to chase, thus working over the race leader's team.

Gentlemen in Brutal Competition

As with most endeavors, there is a social aspect to mass-start bicycle racing. Etiquette, politics, and interpersonal relations often play a part in racing. Monkey around too much, and the competition remembers—if not later in the day, then the next stage, or during the next race. And the racers are talking amongst themselves while they're racing. When it comes to attacking or chasing, there are plenty of informal deals being made. And because the Tour is bicycle racing's biggest stage, dirty tricks or double-dealing will be reported around the world—which is not only bad for the individual, but his team's sponsors.

As a result, racers often give lip service to (and some actually believe) in that murky conceit known as sportsmanship. Playing fair, helping others, winning and losing graciously are part of that. And it often does have an impact on the racing. Racers don't want to be seen attacking in response to a favorite crashing, flatting, heeding the call of nature, or picking up a musette bag in the feed zone. Succeeding with this tactic can forever leave a black mark by one's success and can result in payback. And being a gracious winner is usually important; it's typical to see someone who is about to don yellow let his fellow breakaway riders fight for the stage win while he rolls in behind. Racers who are friends outside of racing claim to be happy when their friend succeeds.

Strategies for the Stages

Each kind of stage and each set of conditions offers a different challenge; thus, different tactics are needed. Sometimes, the smart thing is to expend every last calorie of energy while other times, it's smarter to hold something back. What follows is a rundown of how certain kinds of stages at particular moments in the race call for different tactics and elicit different styles of racing.

Prologue Most Tours start with a prologue. The several-kilometer race against the clock is an appetizer, a way to rank the riders before the race really begins the next day. Rarely are the few seconds gained or lost by the favorites critical in the end, but that doesn't mean that people will be taking it easy. The smallest margin of victory in the history of the Tour is eight seconds: the gap between Greg LeMond and Laurent Fignon after the final stage in 1989. And since team classification, best young rider classification, and points classification—in addition to the stage win and overall classification—start with the prologue, there is reason for just about everyone to be giving their all in the prologue.

And even if racers know they can't win or come close in the prologue, it's still in their own and their team's interest to race as hard as possible. Their placing could make a difference on a later date. But there are generally two groups of riders expected to do well in the prologue, and the attention is generally focused on them. The obvious group are the GC riders. The big favorites want to start distancing themselves from their rivals, or at least deal a psychological blow, while the long shots want to limit their losses.

The second group is the time trial specialists. This group only gets a few stages where they can showcase their specialty. Even within the time trialists, there are people who are better at prologues. These riders are often former track racers who specialized in the pursuit. The pursuit is two riders starting on opposite sides of the track going head-to-head for 4 km. The short distance is all about keeping focus through the searing pain, as the margin of victory at the highest level is often a second or two.

There is still intense racing behind these two groups. The sprinters want to limit their losses to the yellow jersey, no matter who it is. They want to lose as few seconds as possible because they and their team plan on winning as many intermediate sprints as possible in the next few days so a sprinter can take yellow, if only for a little while.

Domestiques supporting the favorites will also want to give full gas at the prologue. The upcoming team time trial employs a traditional time trial starting order. The lowest-ranked team goes first; the highest, last. The team classification based on the prologue is often still the ranking at the time of the team time trial, so each favorite will have at least two team members going for it as well.

Each pre-race favorite also has a *domestique* who will function as his rabbit for the time trial. This rider is usually the second-fastest time trialist on the team. It is his job to slay himself in the time trial so his assistant team director following in the car behind takes time splits for every kilometer. The race generally takes a few time splits over the length of any time trial. The information will be given to the team director, who will use it to help pace the leader on his time trial effort.

And even the weakest *domestiques* on the weakest teams will be giving the prologue all the stick they can dig up. They might be called upon to put in an early attack in one of the opening stages. If fate smiles upon them, they might be lucky enough to ride that breakaway long enough to pick up time bonuses at the intermediate sprints, win the stage, and finish with enough time in hand to take yellow for a day.

The Opening Stages Traditionally, the Tour starts out with some of the flattest stages of the race. Because just about everyone in the race is only separated by several seconds, just about everyone can rationalize having a go at the *maillot jaune*. This makes for some of the most nervous, and thus dangerous, racing of the Tour. In 2004, there were ninety-nine crashes in the opening week.

These stages are supposed to be showcases for the sprinters. Their teams set them up to gobble the intermediate sprints and the time bonuses that go with them, and shoot for the stage victory at the end. The sprinters who did a decent prologue can, with enough time bonuses in the first few days, ride themselves into the yellow and/or green jerseys. Many of the favorites are happy if they get to hide in the middle of the field, saving energy for stages where they expect to gain or lose time.

Of course, there are few gifts given. There are always teams that don't want to give away stages to the sprinters. These are teams that don't have favored sprinters, or have riders who are good a day or two, but can't recover well enough to contend for overall victory. There is a group of riders known as headbangers; these guys like to break away early in the stage when few are interested in racing hard. They hope to establish a big lead while the rest of the field is taking it easy. And a "big" lead can definitely be significant—up to twenty minutes. If the field encounters some problems along the way, like major crashes or sudden thunderstorms, these headbangers could not only take the stage, but could earn any or all of the leader's jerseys. The first North American to wear yellow, Canada's Alex Steida, won the yellow, white, polka-dot, combination, and green jerseys on one day in 1986.

But the headbanger's getting away is dependent on many things. For one, the group can't be too big. If it's a big breakaway, it's likely that someone is going to want to not do any work. The guys in the break don't want a person who's sucking wheel early; this rider will be saving energy while they're using it at prodigious rates and might be too fresh at the end. They also don't want a rider who's a race favorite or the top lieutenant of a race favorite. Such riders aren't welcome because even if they add tremendous horsepower, they increase the likelihood that the field won't let them get away.

And the field will let some breaks go, but not others. The team that controls the yellow jersey is, by tradition, supposed to control the race. The reasoning is that they will want to hold onto yellow as long as possible, and thus it is their responsibility to keep the breakaways in check. But not all teams are strong enough or have the desire to control the race. Sometimes, the yellow jersey's team decides not to take responsibility for controlling the race.

When the yellow jersey can't or refuses to control the race, particularly in the early stages, the teams with the leading sprinters generally take over. They should want to win all the intermediate sprints and the stage so they can put their sprinter in yellow or green. So the sprinters' teams will either keep the pace of the race so high that no one will get away—which is the strategy when they want to get their man up in the general classification or points standings—or let the break dangle when they want to protect their man wearing the yellow or green jersey.

Meanwhile, the riders in the breakaway have some choices to make. Expect that they're making deals with one another depending on their goals (technically against the rules, but this is a rule that never seems to be enforced). One might want to win the KoM points offered on the course, another the sprint points, another wants to make time on the field. If they can trust one another and feel they're evenly matched, chances are the break will work smoothly together. If the breakaway riders don't make a point of trying to win intermediate sprints, they've probably agreed to share the spoils and concentrate on winning the stage.

Back in the field, the teams have to decide if they want the break to work or get caught—and if they do want the break caught, when. Pro racers are experienced enough that they can generally tell what kind of gap to let the breakaway have, like up to twenty minutes, before they start bringing it back. The teams chasing probably want to catch the breakaway close to the finish because that makes it easier to control the race and guarantees that everyone finishes together and with a giant sprint.

Everyone knows this, so the breakaway has to work well together in order to stay away. If there are too many passengers (wheelsuckers, people refusing to help the breakaway advance) or sprinters in the break, someone will try to attack the breakaway late in the race. Part of the move is to improve the odds of winning by shedding the weak, unwilling, or unlucky; part of the move is to stay away. The closer the finish gets, the more likely it is that people will start acting in a way that suits their interest in winning. Someone who thinks he can outsprint the others will stop pulling at the front. Someone who thinks he can't sprint will start attacking. And so the cat-and-mouse tactical games begin.

Those back in the field chasing also are aware of the tactical possibilities. Generally, in the final kilometers, one or two teams that have an outstanding sprinter will race to the front and try to make the race as fast as possible. The teams create "trains," using every rider they have to deliver their favored sprinter to the final two hundred to three hundred meters at the front, and in the shelter of at least one teammate. The teams will line up single file and each rider will ride until exhaustion—not a hard thing to reach after 100 miles when accelerating up to 35 mph—at which point they'll make a gesture, usually a flick of the elbow, to the teammate behind, swing off, and drift backwards. Sometimes, two teams will line up next to each other and basically have a giant drag race over the final kilometers to get their sprinter in the best position.

Behind the trains, there are other sprinters jockeying for position. Some have great sprints but don't have a team to support them. Some lost teammates due to bad luck. But these guys will be sitting behind the trains, looking for their opportunity.

And near the other sprinters are a few other riders who are hoping the trains will have mistimed their efforts. If a sprinter's train incorrectly gauged the distance to the finish, the pace of the field might suddenly let up. At this gasp, a few literally last-minute opportunists might attack, hoping that the other riders won't waste their final effort to bring them back. They might launch themselves in the last kilometer of the race hoping that the field will pause just long enough that they can squeak out the stage win.

For most of the first week, since the time gaps and points differences are close, most of the stages will have these elements.

Team Time Trial The team time trial, which always takes place in the first week, is a brutally hard event that is generally regarded as the second big test of the favorites.

The event was dropped from the Tour in the mid-1990s, and came back in 2000. The concept is pretty simple: Each team lines up together and is sent off in several-minute intervals on an identical course. It isn't a race that the uninitiated fan can easily appreciate, but for the *tifosi*, it's a great spectacle.

The time for the team is taken on the fifth rider to finish. All riders who finish together are given the same time and have that time added to their total. If there are riders who get dropped by their team, they have to race as hard as they can to get to the finish before the time cut is enforced, which is a percentage off the slowest finish time. Also, the team's time is added to their team gc total.

Race favorites with weak teams hate this event, while the favorites with strong teams love it. It is a chance to take or lose several minutes on the competition. All teams have to be concerned with losing riders. They have to decide whether it is more important to lose anywhere from a few seconds to a few minutes to their competition or lose a *domestique* who could help later.

There are also teams that will decide how hard they'll ride depending on where their top rider currently figures on the overall classification. A team with a rider who could possibly take yellow before the mountains will ride at their limit to keep him in the hunt for yellow. The team that possesses the yellow jersey will give their all to keep the jersey for another day.

Possibly to limit the advantage of Armstrong's team, possibly just to give poor time-trialing climbers a better chance of doing well, ASO decided to limit the time gained and lost during the team time trial in 2004. While the winner set the fastest time, the second-place team, no matter how much slower, was awarded a time only twenty seconds behind; third, forty seconds; and so on down to the final team. The rule isn't liked by everyone and the rule may be changed if the change is thought to be beneficial to keeping the race close.

Mid-Mountain Stages These kinds of stages are sometimes served up as hors d'ouvres the day or two before the first real mountain stage. Mid-mountain often means really hilly, without the hills going over major mountain passes. On stages like this, there are usually a series of moderate climbs situated near the end of the stage. While the favorites often watch each other, playing a game of shadowing and feints, fearing that too big an effort will result in a bad ride on a major mountain stage, an enterprising rider or two might take off in a breakaway to grab the yellow jersey for a day or two of glory before the real climbing begins.

Mountain Stages The race changes on the first mountain stage. The sprinters and most of the stars of the first week are no longer racing for the yellow jersey or the stage win, but to survive. They'll have another chance to shine by the end of the race, provided they can get over the mountains.

It's a new race. Those hoping to win have to show their faces in the mountains. And on the long, often steep climbs, there is only so much a team can do to protect their leader. There are also specialist climbers who come out to play. Some will be going for stage wins, while others have hopes of winning the climber's jersey or getting onto the podium.

Teams vying for victory in the team general classification also have to do well in the mountains, so each of these teams will try to have at least three riders at the front each day through the mountains. And the sprinters who can climb decently will try to hang with the climbers as long as possible so they can win intermediate sprints before the final climb of the day.

There is still the specter of the long breakaway. A small group often gets a gap early in the stage. These people might be there in hopes of winning the stage, but just as likely, they're interested in scoring both sprint points and KoM points. Since the bigger climbs offer more points for crossing the summit first, the climbing competition has finally started to attract the climbers. But, since there are more points up for grabs on the later climbs of any day, the break has to be in front for most of the stage in order for the escape to be worthwhile.

Another strategy that comes into play on the mountain stages is sort of a combination defensive and offensive ploy. A team that has one of the favorites in good position, but not in yellow, might try to send a rider or two up the road early in a mountain stage. This could force the yellow jersey's team to chase. And then, after much of the chasing, the favorite attacks the race leader and tries to catch up with his teammates down the road. If he makes contact, the *domestiques*, who have been racing at the front all day, then ride even harder to help their leader increase his lead.

The race favorites usually try to use their team very carefully in the mountains. The riders who are only average climbers set the pace up the mountains for their leader early in the stage and then drop back. The riders who are good climbers are saved so they can aid their leader on the final climb or two of the day. It will be their job to keep a steady pace for their leader if he gets dropped by the other climbers, or, if their leader is feeling good, they'll set a hard tempo for the leader so the other climbers can get dropped.

All of this strategy is happening while the race profile is most severe. For those who get dropped by the leaders, it is usually their duty to finish the day so they can start the next day. Maybe they've crashed, maybe they're battling a virus. Maybe they simply bonked, but at a certain point, they have to go into conservation mode and do what it takes to survive. They might be feeling better tomorrow, and their team will need them.

On every mountain stage, there's a group of riders who are just trying to make it to the finish within the time cut.

This group is known as the *grupetto* in Italian, *l'autobus* in French, and sometimes "the laughing group." There are moments when they can have fun, but their job is to make it to the finish within the time limit and by conserving as much effort as possible. There is usually a "driver," an older pro who is good at determining what kind of pace the group needs to make in order to finish in time. There is no attacking, and the pace is as steady as they can make it. This usually means that the pace is such that everyone can hang on going up the mountains, and then they ride hard down the mountains and on the flats in between.

Still, sometimes a little extra help is essential to survival. Riders have been known to hang onto the side of follow cars and accept pushes from fans when the mountains are steep.

Rest Day There are two rest days in every Tour. They're usually placed after each mountain range has been covered. Resting means they aren't racing, but most are riding. The teams put in a ride of two or three hours to keep their legs and bodies moving. Usually, those racing well lament the rest day, while those struggling express relief.

Between the Mountains Often, there are a few stages placed between the Alps and the Pyrenees. While the favorites might try to make up for some time lost in the mountains, they usually want to save their energy for the second mountain range. Usually, riders who have no hopes of winning the race or one of the jersey competitions try to get away early on these stages. They frequently have company from teams that are in the hunt for the lead in the team general classification. Once the break is away, the yellow jersey's team generally rides tempo for the rest of the day, letting the break stay away, but keeping the gap such that none of the attacking riders pose a threat to the top of the overall leader board.

The Second Mountain Range The racing is once again full-on, though the number of contenders has been dramatically reduced. While the racing doesn't get physically easier, the tactical permutations are often fewer, as far less people have a chance of riding into the golden fleece. The second range is the last real chance for the race leader to be challenged, for the lead to change in the climbers' competition, for the mountain goats to showcase their skills, for teams vying for team gc to play a few more hands of poker.

While the team of the leader will try to keep an iron grip on the race, they'll let race-long attacks go up the road, provided there's no threat to the race lead. Often, a team leader who fell out of contention in the first mountain range wants to show he still has some fight in his legs. So long as he's way down on time, he's allowed to go.

The pace of racing is often different through the second mountain range. Phonak's Floyd Landis has found the first range often means stages are raced all-out all day, while the second range means the stage pace starts slower but ramps up higher at the end.

Final Flat Stages With the outcome of the general classification usually all but certain, the top riders are looking for steady days in the saddle. They're happy to let a breakaway filled with lowly-ranked riders take the day. The breakaway usually means that the *peloton* will ride steadily behind with the yellow jersey's team setting the pace for the field.

However, the riders who are trying to take the green jersey off the points leader want the field to stay together as long as possible so they can take points at the intermediate sprints. Often, the points competition is decided in the last few days of the race, so every sprint counts.

And the team general classification could change with a breakaway as well, so teams going for team gc have to be on the lookout for the opportunities to take and lose times.

Occasionally, the overall standings are still very close going into the final time trial. This happened in 2003, and challenger Jan Ullrich tried to gain some seconds on yellow jersey–holder Armstrong on the days between the final mountains and the final time trial. He tried to sneak off with an intermediate sprint, but Armstrong was vigilant and also got a time bonus.

Final Time Trial The final time trial of the race usually occurs on the penultimate stage. Few have incentive to go hard, so most of the racers do the time trial only as hard as necessary to finish within the time cut and start the final stage.

Three groups of riders are racing the last time trial as hard as they can. The first group is the top twenty on the general classification. The difference between a good ride and bad will be several minutes, which is enough to gain or lose places on the overall classification. Because of this carrot, the top riders of the race are the favorites to win the stage. The second group is the time trial specialists. This is their last chance to win. The third group consists of the top time trial riders on teams trying to win the team gc. Teams vying for this win will have "saved" their three best time trial riders for this day.

Beyond the glory of chasing victories are the top *domestiques* of the leaders. These guys will race the time trial at their limit under the watchful eye of a team director, thereby providing kilometer-by-kilometer time checks for their bosses to base their own rides on. Often, it is their job to try to race to their limit a few kilometers before the finish so the boss has a faster time to shoot for.

The Champs-Elysées The final stage always takes the riders into Paris, where they race around the Champs-Elysées for several laps before finishing on the famed avenue. The race for the overall is almost always decided before this stage starts—and the challengers usually state they're not going to attack the race leader—so the opening kilometers are ridden easily and the riders make a point of enjoying the ride. While the intermediate sprints force the riders to pick up the pace, racing really begins once the riders take the first lap on the Champs-Elysées.

While there are plenty of attacks, the race usually finishes in a mass sprint, one final flourish for the sprinters who suffered through the mountains. Sometimes, the points competition comes down to the finish of the stage, the last sprint of the Tour. This happened in 2003, where Baden Cooke finished one place ahead of Robbie McEwen and won the green jersey by two points.

In 2005, it looked like the points competition would once again be decided by the final sprint on the Champs-Elysées. But Alexandre Vinokourov surprised everyone by winning the first intermediate sprint and attacking the field in the final kilometers to win solo. Vinokourov was out to move up from sixth to fifth on gc, and the time bonuses gave him the margin to move up a spot on the final day.

8

LE CARAVANE PUBLICITAIRE

Le caravane publicitaire, unseen to most of the world, is an essential element of the Tour. While its original function was simply to pay the bills, it is now integral to the celebration of France that is the Tour.

When Henri Desgrange decided to rid the Tour de France of trade teams and solo *touriste-routiers* in favor of national teams and regional teams in 1930, he needed to find a new way to pay for race expenses. Besides raising fees for host towns, he created *le caravane publicitaire*, the publicity caravan. It was to be a convoy of cars paid for by firms who wanted to advertise during the race. They would travel ahead of the race, using whatever means they could to tell people about their product.

It was an inspired creation. At first, it started with only ten companies paying for cars, but it quickly grew to forty-six cars within five years. Added sponsors helped dramatically boost prize money, from a total of 150,000 francs in 1929 (the year before the caravan was added), to 800,000 francs in 1937, and the winner that year received 200,000 francs. These additional sponsors also advertised in *L'Auto*, boosting the paper's ad revenue as well. Reflecting on this success, Desgrange said, "If the publicity caravan did not exist, we would have to create it." In Desgrange's mind, at least, having the sponsors drive ahead of the race kept the race itself pure, not sullied by outside influences, keeping with the directive that the race be decided on its merits.

In the 1950s, the race finally gave in to the idea of "extra *sportifs*," noncycling sponsors getting involved in the sponsorship of teams, even though race director Jacques Goddet worried, "To see French champions transformed into sandwich-board men by extra *sportif* interests . . . we cannot let that happen." He relented, and the riders are certainly sandwich-board men today, though it's hard to find anyone complaining about it.

Even though the national team–format Tours have been gone for over forty years, thanks partially to the extra *sportifs*, the caravan has stayed. For one thing, the revenue was too good to pass up. The roads were already closed, so they didn't take up any space. And it added to the festival atmosphere that the Tour creates for the public lining the roads—a win-win for everybody.

The Tour as a Spectator Sport

Each year, an estimated 15 million spectators line the roads of the Tour. That's an average of 714,286 spectators a day, or more than 4,000 per kilometer. And the watching often becomes a family activity; more than half of the groups of five or more come with children fifteen years and younger. Tour spectators spend an average of six hours on the roadside, and while it is estimated that people from twenty-two nations come to watch the Tour, most are French—76 percent of the population of

France has seen at least one stage of the Tour over their lifetime. But it's the grueling mountain stages that really capture the world's interest, and the percentage of foreign spectators goes up to 30 percent during the fierce uphill stages of the race.

There are many things about watching a stage of the Tour that are easy—no one has to pay for tickets or drive to a stadium—but they have found that the average spectator has traveled 100 km from their home to see the race. And these people aren't going for a few innings or packing it in during the third quarter, they're staying all day—a tailgate party where the event comes right by your trunk or blanket. The race itself takes anywhere from forty-five seconds to forty-five minutes to pass, so there is a captive audience available.

But for the spectators, the caravan and the resulting spectacle are sometimes as much of a draw as the race itself. Before the idea of the caravan was hatched, there were already sponsored vehicles in the race. Bayard Alarms, Lion Noir Polish, and Meunier Chocolates were already in the caravan, but they were in the convoy of vehicles behind the race. Putting them before the race gave the vehicles a bigger audience. And they enticed the audience with goodies tossed out of the cars to the fans on the side of the road. Meunier Chocolates threw out chocolates and paper flags, which the fans were only too happy to snatch up. The flags were for waving, and probably were distributed for the same reason such stuff is distributed today—not only is it a keepsake with a memorable logo, but the holding and waving is good for brand recognition, inspiring frenzy, and getting caught on camera.

Naturally, the caravan created its own competition, where sponsors treated their cars like competitive floats in a Mardi Gras parade. The object isn't so much to win, but to catch the most eyes, distribute the most product, ultimately experiencing the maximum bounce for the advertising effort.

The vehicles created are outlandish, and there is always some kind of stunt going on. In the 1930s, a magician had a car in the caravan. French accordianist and singer Yvette Horner played atop a car in the 1940s and '50s, which helped grow her fan base. She was popular in her era, though today some critics say her popularity was largely due to her performances at the Tour.

The products advertised have been largely mundane. Chocolates, mail order catalogues, pens, supermarkets, tires, newspapers, sausages, etc.—the kinds of products people use every day. But despite the ordinary products, the vehicles are extraordinary. The caravan isn't just painted-up cars, but motorcycles, roadsters, vans, trucks . . . any vehicle that has a motor and can convey a message.

The Caravan

The caravan is huge, consisting of two hundred plus vehicles, representing forty-five brands. It takes forty-five minutes to pass, and this mammoth procession happens every day of the race, over every kilometer of road the Tour uses, in all weather. The caravan must remain at least two hours ahead of the race, so it takes masterful planning and direction to keep it on schedule. There is a caravan director who has radio contact as well as GPS coordinates for each car, and two motorcycles to make sure his directions are heard and heeded. It's a noisy, swag-handing procession that is playing music, announcing news, enacting scenes on floats, waving to crowds, and distributing stuff.

The swag-distribution can be the highlight of the procession for many, and the caravan shouldn't disappoint; ASO estimates that 11 million "gifts" were handed out in 2004. Many report having seen a senior citizen knock over a kid in a dash for the swag, often a cap or keychain.

Many of the vehicles belong to major sponsors of the

race. There are four levels of official sponsorship of the race, and often these sponsors have a vehicle in the caravan. The top level is "Tour de France Club members," which included Champion Supermarkets, Credit Lyonnais, Nestlé Aquarel, and Skoda Auto in 2005, though all have signed long-term contracts. Credit Lyonnais has been with the Tour for at least a generation. All have vehicles in the caravan, and two sponsor competitions. Credit Lyonnais sponsors the yellow jersey and the team classification, and, as of 2004, put €4.35 million Euros into sponsorship. Champion sponsors the climber's jersey. Nestlé provides drinks to the *peloton* and public, and Skoda provides cars for the Tour. Below this level are the official partners who spend between €1 million and €2 million, then official suppliers, who pay at least €350,000.

Since the Tour is seen around the world, it makes sense that many of the sponsors are multinational corporations who aren't only appealing to the French, but at least all of Europe, if not the world. Still, many of the sponsors in the caravan are certainly domestic and aimed at the French market, such as Cochonou sausages, Haribo candies, and Brioche la Boulangeres breads (baked goods for supermarkets).

Most race sponsors have vehicles in the caravan, though some are present as technical support and some are there for the riders. It certainly helps the Tour to have a watch company, currently Festina, paying for the timing; a computer company, CSC, taking care of the computers, and a motorcycle company, Kawasaki, taking care of the motorcycles.

All have an angle for the caravan. Credit Lyonnais has cars and go-carts with a giant lion theme, the symbol of the bank. They also toss out hats, pens, keychains, and even bags for people to put the stuff in. And at award presentations, they give out stuffed Lyonnais Lions for riders to hold up on the podium, highly coveted by riders, though Tyler Hamilton was known to give them to his golden retriever. Skoda tosses out logoed sun hats, baseball hats, and keychains, among other things.

Aquarel might have one of the largest presences in the caravan. They put fifteen vehicles in the caravan and publish a daily free paper called *Eaufficial of the Tour de France*, which has a circulation of 30,000 and deals with non-sport issues of the race.

Entertainment might also be considered as one of their methods. Six of the fifteen vehicles are decorated around themes: A clown float, a "Doctor Miracle" float, a "grocery" float, a "just married" float, and perhaps one of the more controversial floats, a "Fire Brigade," which douses the public—it's loved on hot days, so long as people aren't near their food. They also have roadsters designed to look like their bottle. Through the vehicles, they distribute 500,000 bottles of Aquarel. They are small (33 cl) bottles and as Aquarel's spokesperson points out, it takes skill to get the bottles to people by the side of the road safely.

And that isn't all. They also have huge Aquarel arches at the "25 km to go" point in each stage and Aquarel banners on fences at the side of the road wherever possible. This ensures that most of the people watching the race on television see the company logo.

Also in the caravan is Haribo, a maker of gummi bears. They've been in the caravan since 1999, distributing bags of candy every day, as well as sponsoring daily events by the start or finish line. The event is called *"L'Etape du Enfants,"* The Kid's Stage. There are toboggan-type slides, bicycle obstacle courses, and even bicycle races—on stationary bikes. Between the caravan and the Kid's Stage, they distribute over 1.5 million "mini bags" of candy during the Tour.

Not that others don't offer food. A pretzel-maker had cars in the caravan, and they shared bags of pretzels with the fans. Cochonou, a French sausage-maker (owned by Sara Lee), puts several vintage-looking Citröens into the caravan. All have an open top, and are painted like a red-and-white-checked tablecloth. Women stand in the back and toss out plastic-wrapped sausages. Many, if not most, are caught and eaten, though more than a few have been seen acting as missiles and bopping people in the head. Cochonou claims they see sales increase 30 percent between June and August compared to the rest of the year.

Since most of the caravan is never seen beyond the French roadside, smaller national brands are typical. In 2001, three cars cost €20,000, so it is an advertising method within reach of smaller companies as well. And with fifteen million people taking a good look at a logo and fighting for a sample or trinket, name recognition can grow tremendously over the course of three weeks.

Not all of the caravan ideas and samples are so practical for the fans. If no one has a particularly good idea of what to do, the giant float seems to be the sensible backup. Official sponsor PMU, which sponsors the green jersey competition, is a pari-mutuel betting concern. They have cars with giant papier-mâché–style jockey-bestridden horses in full gallop bolted to the roof. They also toss out giant green hands for people to wear and wave as the Tour races by. Champion supermarkets has a giant cyclist in a polka-dot jersey on the roof of their cars.

The Tour itself sells newspapers and magazines in the caravan as well. After all, this is a sporting event that was founded by a newspaper, and in fact it is still closely tied to three major French publications: *L'Équipe*, *Le Parisien*, and *Vélo*. People can buy a package of newspapers and magazines to catch up on their Tour and news reading as the caravan goes by so they're up on the Tour news before the race reaches them.

Some of the biggest trade unions in France also have a presence in the caravan. The moving space is presented free of charge by ASO, to give unions a chance to get their messages out. CGT and their newspaper *La*

Nouvelle Vie ouvrière, Force *ouvrière's FO Hebdo*, and CFTC's *La Vie à defender* all have cars in the caravan where they can promote their unions and causes. They usually hand out newspapers on the roads.

While this is a good gesture that demonstrates the Tour is responsive to the need of French trade unions, some see it as a way of buying support. Since they have cars in the caravan, the unions are less likely to use a strike tactic—one that has caused the Tour occasional problems—on the race as a way to get attention for a cause. The counterargument is that most unions would not want the negative publicity that would come with disrupting a race known the world over.

Prizes and Surprises

The podium presentations are a favorite part of the pageantry of the Tour de France. A rider gets a trophy, flowers, and kisses on both cheeks from silent spokes-models referred to as Podium girls. The girls themselves are dressed for the occasion, wearing a uniform that reflects the sponsor of the prize they are awarding. The flowers are traditional and the trophy usually a design that calls attention to the sponsor. The podium itself is part of the sponsorship package, with sponsor names plastered around and a backdrop that reflects the logo and jersey theme.

The presentation itself is usually done as quickly as possible after the stage has been completed. The podium is often right next to the finish line, and late-finishing riders have to dodge the scrum standing by the platform. The stage winner gets his trophy, bouquet, and kisses, then the yellow, green, polka-dot, and white jersey competition leaders get awarded fresh jerseys for their efforts, complete with their own podium girls and sponsor-coordinated background.

This is all business for two reasons. One is timing. Tour officials want these images available as quickly as possible to the press. Another is commerce. The presentations reflect most of the biggest sponsorship agreements of the race, so the sponsors have to get what they're paying for.

What is less known, and rarely seen outside of the region where the stage is finishing, are the regional prizes. Well off the official prize lists, and rarely found in race reports, these have no particular relevance to the world at large, and there are no rules concerning what can and can't be offered, but they reflect on both the race, the region, and why the Tour is part of the fabric of French life. The racers always appreciate a little something extra, which can not only line their pockets, but give them more press mentions. and the locals want to highlight their region with a favorite product.

The prizes given often seem whimsical and fun, with an odd provenance. In 2004, when the race visited Amiens, there was a prize for the best-placed rider from the area. Lamballe gave a horse to the Portugese rider Jose Azevedo (he is from Lamballe's sister city in Portugal). Richard Virenque won a cow for winning the stage to St. Flour. Lannemezan gave Ivan Basso a black pig for winning the stage to La Mongie. Annemasse gave Gilberto Simoni a trophy and a big wheel of cheese for being the first rider to crest the Col de la Madeleine (winning the KoM on the Madeleine also meant scoring the cash prize known as the Souvenir Henri Desgrange, for the first person over the highest climb of the race). In Besançon, every racer received a clock, a specialty of the region.

These regional prizes are different every year. In other years, expect porcelain, champagne, cheese, more livestock, coffee, wine, vases, and whatever else the regional people can think up. Since these awards are not part of the race sponsorship and reflect where the race is passing through, the awards don't happen on the podium after the stages, but in the morning before the stages begin. The atmosphere is more relaxed, as the clock hasn't started and racers are just digesting their food rather than anxious to get out of sweaty Lycra and move on to the necessary job of eating.

Which is just as well. Many of the fans along the road are doing the same thing at the end of the stage: finishing up the last bottle of wine, packing up the picnic, and either rolling home or moving on to the next spot of road to call their own for the next day.

9

THE TECH TOUR

The Tour is the ultimate proving ground for bicycles. Ever since the race began, there has been an arms war in bike technology. First, to get the bikes to the finish safely without breaking; then to add gears, lighten up, and improve aerodynamics—all to give sponsored riders an edge.

Naturally, the founder of the Tour hated the march of technology. Henri Desgrange wanted the race decided on the merits of the riders, not their bicycles. He opposed most improvements that occurred during his tenure as race director, only reluctantly allowing them into the race.

In 1903, bikes were high-tech marvels, so impressive that cars, motorcycles, and airplanes were borrowing bicycle technology—and a number of companies that became mainstays in those fields started in the bike business. The basic shape of the bike was fairly well established by 1903, and bikes of that era look similar to bicycles of today. Early Tour bikes had a "diamond" frame, pneumatic tires, tensioned spoked wheels, curved handlebars, and a single, fixed gear that was used both to advance the bicycle and slow it down. Handbrakes were a rarity. The pedals usually had toe clips, but not straps. The wheels had nuts holding them to the bike. While the average bicycle of this era might have weighed around forty pounds, racing bikes were frequently less than thirty pounds . . . and there's a good chance the racers of the Tour were competing on twenty-five-pound bikes. The machines were dazzlingly modern for the time . . . but they carried an almost unfathomable amount of extra weight by today's standards.

When aluminum rims first appeared in 1926, an improvement over the wooden rims of the day, Desgrange thought them too dangerous. He banned derailleurs (gear-shifting mechanisms), claiming they made cycling too easy. A racer who dared to use a derailleur in 1936 was docked a ten-minute penalty. Desgrange so disliked the influence of technology on his race that he took to issuing standard frames to the riders for many years. He abandoned this policy and then returned to it before his reign was over.

But the bicycle had to move forward; not only because racers were looking for an edge, but because bicycle companies were trying to improve their wares and distinguish themselves from the pack to better sell their products to the public. Everyone wants a bike that's better than their last; no one can disagree with improvements that add to efficiency and comfort.

Freewheels were the first technological improvement to come to tour riders' bikes. While freewheels (toothed cogs with pawls that allow a rider to coast instead of continually pedaling) had been invented in the 1890s, the need to coast wasn't an apparent advantage until big mountains had to be descended. This upgrade became common in 1906. With coasting, handbrakes became essential. At first, brakes slowed down the bike by rubbing against the top of tires, but by 1910, caliper brakes were making their way onto race bikes.

Other cycling innovations were a bit slower to catch on at the Tour. The standard bolted-on wheels typically used on the first bicycles (and still found on today's track bikes) were slow to change and necessitated a wrench. Wing nuts were faster, and appeared on bikes in the early 1900s. But as bike technology advanced, changing tires with nuts and bolts proved cumbersome. The advent of the quick release lever to fasten or remove the wheels was a huge leap forward in bike technology. Invented by Tullio Campagnolo, it was born out of failure and exemplifies how many bicycle innovations came about—a tinkering rider had a problem, saw a need, and figured out a way to address that need. Campagnolo got a flat in a race, and his hands were too cold to work the wing nuts. That race was lost, but the world benefitted. This single invention, the quick-release lever, showed up the same year as derailleurs were allowed in the Tour.

Interestingly, while technological improvements used to come slowly to the Tour, now they come quickly. As recently as 1989, racers were waiting for others to test new gadgets before racing with them. Nowadays, the cutting-edge stuff gets to the Tour before it goes to market, though it gets to market pretty fast.

The Derailleur

The derailleur has been nearly universal on adult bicycles for many years. The device derails the chain off of one cog or chainring and pushes it onto another, thus shifting gears. This helps make for comfortable pedaling at a wide range of speeds—and thus speeding up racers and races. Light and reliable, one can now find up to ten cogs in the back of the bike and up to three chainrings in front. But when derailleurs first appeared, they were not reliable and took tremendous skill to use. Component makers were still playing around with designs. Many racers went for the reliability of changing the gears by hand rather than taking a chance on the new technology of derailleurs.

Hard to say if it was the improvement of derailleurs or the retirement of Desgrange that saw derailleurs enter the Tour in 1937. The parallelogram design that is used with all rear derailleurs today was not the design first used, though it won out by the 1950s, when the parallelogram front derailleur became common as well.

Lightness

Weight has always been an issue with bicycles. The less weight one has to carry uphill and while accelerating, the easier it is for the riders. But weight has to be balanced against durability. A bike that can't take the punishment that racers and roads put out simply isn't useful. As many a Tour rider has discovered, a disabled bike can be the difference between winning and finishing.

As technology has improved (and the roads have become better) over the past century, bike parts have become lighter and more durable. In the early 1970s, it seemed like everyone was drilling out bike parts to lighten them up. Crankarms, brake levers, calipers, derailleurs, seatposts, were all put under a drill to remove excess metal. In some cases, this threatened the integrity of the design, leading to an increased risk of failure. Then, at the end of the 1970s and into the early 1980s, durability became the most-desired quality, so drilling became passé.

For awhile in the early 1990s, it seemed that technological advancement had slowed in the bike world—or even backslid. Top racers were winning some of the toughest races on designs that wouldn't have even been considered cutting-edge eight years earlier. But soon, this period was followed by a cycle of technological advances. Titanium frames showed up, with some dalliances in carbon, then aluminum, then aluminum/carbon, now all-carbon. Parts were tricked-out with titanium pieces as after-market add-ons.

Currently, the UCI has put a limit on how light a bicycle used can be. The limit is now 6.9 kg, or a shade over 15 lbs. And it's a goal that's getting easier and easier to reach—in fact, some bikes come in under that limit, and mechanics have to scramble to make a few parts heavier so the bike will be legal.

It wasn't uncommon in the recent past for the top guy on a team to have a separate climbing bike for the mountain stages of the Tour. In 1986, Hinault, LeMond, and their teammates on the La Vie Claire team switched from steel frames to carbon fiber frames for mountain stages in the Tour, a practice that became more and more common until recently. Now that many bike companies mass-produce ultralight frames, it isn't uncommon for racers to have a super-light bike for all races, though sometimes bigger riders request a heavier frame and wheels because they believe a sturdier bike won't break.

Aero

At one time, getting aerodynamic on a bike meant putting one's handlebars lower and riding the drops with the elbows bent. In the 1970s, riders took to wearing silk jerseys in time trials, thinking silk was more aerodynamic than the standard wool jerseys. Today, many riders test their position and gear in a wind tunnel and can determine, with consultation from aerodynamics experts, which parts and clothing are aerodynamically superior.

Aerodynamic "funny bikes" started to appear in the early 1980s. These bikes looked like arrowheads from the side, had funny-looking upward-sweeping bullhorn-looking handlebars, and were supposed to cut through the wind. The big leap forward was taken by Italian Francesco Moser, who broke the hour record, the most coveted distance record in cycling (as far as one can go in sixty minutes on a velodrome), in 1984 by using an aerodynamic frame and solid "disc" wheels. Success spawns imitators, and within a year, every top competitor had disc wheels for timed events. Competitors selected frame tubing and wheels with a teardrop shape, believing this would make the bikes more "aero."

But most of the aerodynamic resistance to a cyclist comes from the rider, not the bike. Triathletes contributed to the next big advance in aerodynamics—clip-on handlebars. The forward-pointing bars were becoming standard equipment for top triathletes in 1989, when Greg LeMond used them in time trials to win the Tour. The next year, every top racer was time-trialing on them.

Now, pretty much everything a racer uses in a time trial is done with a nod to aerodynamics. Every racer in the Tour has a time-trial bike with a disc wheel in the back, as well as an aero helmet, a skin suit, and even Lycra booties to smooth out the aerodynamic drag cycling shoes create. Most of the improvements in timing are now incremental, but that doesn't mean an advance thought up by a racer, tinkerer, or engineer isn't around the next corner. While racers followed triathletes by a few years in the 1980s, now it is triathletes looking to the Tour to figure out the next aero advance.

Aero vs. Light

The aero needs of road racing are a bit different. Time-trialing is about riding at a steady state. Road racing has plenty of accelerations. Often what is most aero is neither light nor comfortable—which is why aerodynamic time-trial helmets, skinsuits, and time-trial bikes are only used for time trials. And light isn't often aero.

As a result, road bikes are constantly striking a balance between comfort, weight, and aerodynamics. All these three considerations come into play when designing and selecting a wheel; possibly the most important component on a bike in terms of efficiency. Many racers use "deep-dish" wheels on their bike. These wheels have half the spokes of conventional wheels, and the shape is designed to slice through the wind. The problem is that the rim is often heavier than shallower rims. The extra weight is fine once a rider is up to speed, but when he is trying to attack or is attempting a long climb, the added weight can be a severe liability. As a result, racers often have many different sets of wheels—aero wheels for flat stages, and light wheels for climbing stages.

Carbon fiber is fast becoming a popular rim material choice. The material can be made light and fairly strong, which is great. The drawback is that the braking surface often isn't as good or predictable as aluminum. They are also incredibly expensive, but that's not a concern to racers on high-budget teams. Carbon rims might have been the cause of the horrific crash Joseba Beloki of Spain's ONCE team suffered in the 2003 Tour. On a mountain descent, he started to skid, stopped the skid, then his glued-on rear tire popped off the rim. He broke his leg, derailing his career and nearly taking out the best riders in the Tour, who were drafting him.

Repairs on the Road

Technical assistance on the road not only helped speed the race, but also made parts worries a little less serious. Originally, Desgrange wanted the riders to make all the repairs themselves, no matter the size. Of course, the technology of the day meant that fixing a flat could take more than ten minutes; repairing broken parts could take a lot longer. In this era, speeds were lower, packs smaller, and drafting wasn't as important as it is today. Someone could easily come back from a twenty-minute deficit, if for no other reason than his competitors would probably suffer a few flats as well.

Eventually Desgrange relented and assistance was slowly allowed. At first, the rider had to prove he had a problem, so this sometimes meant carrying a broken wheel to a checkpoint as proof. But riders still carried tools, as well as a few spare tires, around their shoulders. As time went on, riders had follow-cars in time trials with spare gear, while they still carried tires and tools for road stages. In 1956, riders became confident enough in the "neutral" support provided by the Tour that many stopped carrying their own spare tires and tools.

Today, each team has two support cars following the race. There's a director driving and a mechanic in the backseat of each car, and not only do they carry wheels and bikes—each rider has an additional bike on one of the two cars—but food, clothing, and tools that should allow them to fix almost anything on the fly. In addition, the teams have a panel truck with extra bikes and parts that travels ahead of the race. There are also neutral support cars and motorcycles patrolling the race, ready to help out any rider with his bike problems.

Stopping is the enemy. Repairs are often made to bikes while riders are still riding them—all it takes is a mechanic leaning out a window. A wheel change should take no longer than ten seconds, and that's a slow change. Five seconds is the goal. Sometimes, taking a spare bike is faster. And, often the bike that the rider gave up is repaired during the race and then given back to him. Mechanics have been spotted climbing out of moving cars to make repairs to bikes lashed on the roof.

Mechanics are an essential element of a cycling team.

Many racers have their own bike workshop at home and are competent mechanics, but at a race, they don't do any wrenching. They might oversee the mechanics' work, or check parts to make sure they're in alignment, but they usually don't touch their bikes between the moment they climb off at the end of a stage, and when they're ready to climb on in the morning.

In the intervening time, every bike is cleaned and checked out. Some are completely taken apart and put back together again—and this often happens when the bike is already in seemingly perfect condition. Anything that looks less than perfect or has some wear is replaced—tires, cogs, chains, brake pads, cables, just about everything. Spare wheels and bikes are checked as well, just to make sure. Things like tires and gear ratios can be changed depending on what the terrain is like for the next day. Don't expect saddles to be changed or their position altered in the least; these venture into the realm of fit issues, and after riding 100 miles a day, the riders can almost always tell when their position is off by even a millimeter. And, because the support cars are literally advertising vehicles, they're washed as well.

The Power of a Mechanic

Mechanics have a say in what riders use. While a contender can make demands on the mechanics in terms of using components they don't approve of, most riders do not have this privilege. Mechanics like reliable parts they don't have to fuss with. If the new component makes their job easier by reducing the amount of time they spend repairing or adjusting or replacing that component, they generally like it. They have to be able to assemble a bike quickly. They like having all the riders using identical gear ratios as well.

As bike production has evolved, maintenance has

become easier. Part of it is that components have been increasingly designed to be easier to install, and to be able to withstand more miles between overhauls. Also, standardization has been employed to an ever-greater number of parts. Many bikes can now be taken apart and put back together with three to four different-sized Allen keys. Since most race frames are made of aluminum, carbon-fiber, or titanium, there are no longer alignment issues. And since few frames are custom-built for a single rider, it's easy to assemble replacements when frames break.

A Tour contender can dictate who touches his bike, and can even have a single mechanic dedicated to the care of his gear. Lance Armstrong has been known to employ a mechanic, who even sleeps with his bikes.

Testing

Many bike designs come about through evolution—cyclists and mechanics shaving a bit here and there, trying a new spring or metal, or working with cycling engineers to get more precise and gain an advantage, however slight. As cycling components have increasingly used new materials, and improvements are harder to eke out, engineers are playing an ever-increasing role in bike design and producing.

A trend noticed in the early 2000s was that pro riders started placing their brake levers higher and higher on their handlebars relative to the "traditional" position. Some handlebar manufacturers did nothing, while others decided to respond. Full Speed Ahead (FSA), a handlebar maker, decided that the riders were on to something, and started making bars that worked better with this new lever position. The innovation was a success with Tour riders as well as other serious riders. This design, and a horde of similar designs, are now on bikes found in the local bike shop.

Because the Tour is the highest-stakes race of the year, most of the products seen at the tour have been tested in training or racing. When a top rider pulls out a "new" bike, it is probably a copy of his old bike with fresh paint. Most team directors and mechanics don't want to risk losing the race on a new or unfamiliar part. It is for this reason that sponsors get equipment to teams and riders ahead of time. The sponsor often has to sell the mechanic on the part as well as the rider, convincing them of the benefits. The riders will use the new equipment in training and decide if they like it enough for *le grand boucle*.

Riders generally want stuff that will help them at their specialty. Climbers want lighter bikes and wheels, time trialists want more aero parts. Big riders often want stronger parts. They're all hoping the parts they get can deliver an edge.

But anything generally has its limits. *Directeur Sportif* Johan Bruyneel told his sponsors that the drop-dead date for new products is the start of the Dauphiné Libéré stage race, one of the final tune-up events before the Tour which takes place in June, less than a month before the tour. This is not an uncommon tactic: The Specialized-sponsored Gerolsteiner team and others have been doing the same thing. If equipment sponsors can't get their riders the latest by the deadline, teams won't allow its use in the Tour. It makes sense; the riders can test it in competition, train on it some more, and then decide whether or not they're comfortable using it in the big dance.

In 1999, back when it was the U.S. Postal Service team, one of Bruyneel's riders crashed and wrecked a wheel. That was enough for the team to decide they couldn't trust that brand of wheels for the rest of the race (even though the wheels were provided by a major sponsor), and they went with another manufacturer.

The Great, Unglamorous Tech Revolutions

With all the gleaming, cutting-edge componentry being improved and refined every year, it's easy to overlook some of the technological advances that have profoundly changed cycling.

Possibly first on the list are the lowly Lycra shorts. They're de rigeur cycling gear around the world today, but twenty-five years ago, people were just switching over from wool. Lycra was a huge step forward in comfort. Jerseys, too, are dramatically lighter and better ventilated than they were twenty years ago.

The electronic cycle computer was first seen at the Tour on Greg LeMond's Gitane bicycle in 1984. Now almost everyone rides with them. Around 1984, heart rate monitors started to be used as a training tool. By 1990, they were becoming common sights in the Tour *peloton*. Sometime after that, power meters started appearing on bikes. In 2005 they were light enough that some people were racing with them at the Tour.

Clipless pedals also started infiltrating the *peloton* in 1985 when Bernard Hinault debuted them at the Tour. Today, so few people know what "toe-clips" are (they're bindings that clip underneath cycling shoes) that the term *clipless* is obsolete. And the pedals caused a revolution in shoes. The shoes are now stiffer in the sole, more comfortable to wear, and more secure in terms of how the binding system works.

Lightweight, plastic sunglasses were debuted by Hinault's teammate LeMond at the 1985 Tour as well. In an ironic twist, Hinault wore metal-framed sunglasses that cut his face in a major crash that year. And in 1986, LeMond brought the first lightweight hard helmet to the

Tour. It was made by Giro, and the helmets seem to get better ventilated every year.

Shimano's brake/shift lever combo, the SIS (Shimano Integrated System), debuted at the Tour in 1990 when everyone else was running downtube shifters. Campagnolo soon followed with their own version. Nowadays few people know what downtube shifters are.

Spy vs. Spy

Some teams take their research and development very seriously. They want to have an edge on their competitors, so they try to hide their own prototype gear for as long as possible while trying to spy on other teams' prototypes. The shadow games usually take the form of sidling over to a team's encampment at a race and trying to take a picture or take measurements of anything that looks new and different. In order to protect their gear, mechanics will hide the team's time-trial equipment in a truck until the last moment before it's ridden, then hide it again the moment the new bike, wheel, handlebar, etc. has finished the race.

Many of these cloak-and-dagger tactics have to do with time-trial equipment. If someone has a new idea and can turn it into a frame, wheel, handlebar, or helmet design, there is a limited window in which the new piece of equipment can be faster and or lighter than everyone else's. So the few to many seconds at time-trial speeds are saved, so long as no one else can get a good look at the new bright idea. Once it is unveiled at the Tour, the finest engineering minds in the bike business will see it and try to learn from it. If they can't suss it out from observation, they'll try to buy the new, fast part in a store, and analyze it in their own wind tunnel or chop it up in their shop to understand what the part does, and how.

Product Rollout

The more ambitious bike companies will debut next year's product at the Tour. Since the Tour is the biggest media event in the cycling world, any exposure in the Tour works as advertising, which can cut both ways. Having a high-profile rider crash out of the Tour because a part failed could be terrible for the manufacturer, but winning any stage, getting exposure in breakaways, or having some of the thousand cycling journalists examine the new widget, wheel, or frame could help create interest from the bike industry, which has trade shows in the fall, or the cycling public, which is often on the lookout for new, cool stuff.

The European pro *peloton* is a hugely important marketing tool. Most of the bike companies that get involved in sponsoring a Pro Tour team see the entire world as their market. Cannondale has used their teams to grow an impressive market share in Europe. Trek, thanks to Lance Armstrong, sees itself as a worldwide brand. Specialized says half their sales are in Europe.

It's almost impossible for a new company to get a heretofore unseen part onto a bike in the Tour. Most teams have contracts with companies to provide every single part they use, and violating the terms of a contract is never a good thing. However, some parts do slip through. Zipp Speed Weaponry, known mostly for their carbon-fiber rims, found themselves a stealth supplier of top riders. Since the cyclists had contracts to ride other gear, the riders would pay for rims, and then have them built up either unlabeled or with a label of the official wheel supplier.

And the stickering of parts is important. There are teams that have technical representatives at the Tour, keeping a relationship with their sponsored teams, learning about the good and bad, advising on proper use and maintenance, and making sure that stickers identifying the product are clearly visible in case the bike is photographed or videotaped.

From the Tour to the Shop Floor

At first, because of necessity, what was ridden at the Tour was what was available in bike shops. As time went on, bicycles and components ridden at the Tour became more and more custom, particularly frames. Even when a rider of the 1970s or 1980s was riding a bike that had GITANE OR MERCIER on the downtube, it was just as likely that the bike was built by the rider's favorite frame-builder and painted to look like the sponsor's bikes. When the American Seven-Eleven team rode the Tour, their first bike sponsor was Murray, then Huffy, two supermarket-brand bikes. Underneath the paint, they were usually custom-built Serottas, though sometimes, they were LandSharks and others. Mechanics, too, took to tweaking, filing, shaving, and improving the stock parts with custom concepts.

Into the 1990s and now the twenty-first century, it is common for the bikes and components ridden at the Tour to be available at any decent-sized bike shop. A few things have happened over the years. One important change was the advent of "compact" geometry, pioneered by Giant bicycles. The compact design allowed for fewer frames to fit a wide range of people. In the 1990s, the ONCE team, a powerhouse squad, was always up on the cutting edge of equipment; they picked up Giant as a bike sponsor. Their director liked that the frames were standard, so the riders had less to complain about and the mechanics less to worry about. Also, carbon fiber is a material that's harder to make custom, particularly as companies building in this material are frequently using molds to lay up their material into monocoque frames. But even without this, a number of manufacturers who work in other materials are convinced that their stock frames can fit most people. Cannondale, which only a few years ago was touting its custom frame–building program, is now pushing standard frame sizing for the masses.

Production methods have also been part of this trend. Improvements that ease assembly and remove fine-tuning have worked to improve equipment across the spectrum of bicycle componentry. It has gotten to the point that the highest-tech components often roll off an assembly line just like any other part.

It's kind of amazing that just about anyone can walk into a bike shop and buy a bike identical to the ones that have conquered the Tour, the Giro, the classics, the World Championships. Not too many other sports give this opportunity. And, in a sense, these advances have helped the technology issue go full circle. Since just about everything is available to just about everybody, the race, much like Desgrange wanted, can be decided on the merits of the riders and not the equipment.

10

CATCHING THE TOUR

When Jonathan Boyer became the first American to ride the Tour in 1981, the event barely caused a ripple in the United States. The two American cycling magazines, *Bicycling* (the general-interest publication) and *Vélo-News* (the racing pub) barely devoted any resources to the Tour. *Bicycling* ran a story and photos in the December issue—which went to bed in October. Both magazines used British freelancers to cover the event. *Vélo-News* had them mail the reports from Europe, and got Dutch photographer Cor Vos to mail his photos from Europe. According to former editor Tim Blumenthal, *Vélo-News* split Tour coverage between two issues—in late July for the first half of the Tour, and in August for the second half. He says of those time frames, "It was a different time, and there was no expectation of instant gratification on Tour news."

Those who wanted Tour news faster had few choices. If they lived in a major city, they could probably track down a French daily newspaper, or possibly a French cycling magazine. If not, the only thing they could do was try to find the Tour on shortwave radio. Blumenthal himself tried doing it. "When the weather was right, I could get Radio France International. At 10 A.M. (4 P.M. in France), I could get some signal. Half of the time I could hear it; half the time it was static." And this uneven signal was a bonus of living high on a Vermont hillside.

In 1984, CBS started broadcasting recaps of the Tour on the weekends. The broadcasts were considered innovative because they married the music video concept to sports, and were less martial and more fun than NFL films. TV personality John Tesh, then a former news reporter, was the on-air talent, and he wrote the music that went with the images. He was joined on air by British commentator and journalist Phil Liggett, and the two, along with the director David Michaels, boiled down the action into fairly easy-to-understand plotlines, with theme music reinforcing the story. They won an Emmy award for their work. Tesh later released an album of his Tour themes, which for many years was played at bike races around the United States.

The television coverage offered most American Tour fans their first glimpses of the race. Until this point, they were limited to short news articles and precious few pictures. Since video cassettes were only starting to become a common consumer product, it was still rare to find European cycling movies in VHS format. While American cycling fans were disappointed by how abbreviated the coverage was, many taped the broadcasts and watched them more than they'll admit.

In 1989, ABC took over the American Tour license from CBS. They stepped up the coverage by broadcasting some stages the same day they happened. This turned out to be particularly important, as Greg LeMond won the race on the last day of the Tour.

Going into the 1990s, ABC and their cable sister, ESPN, increased coverage—recaps on broadcast television on the weekend, same-day coverage at night during the week. People were still taping the shows on their VCRs, but an American company called World Cycling Productions created videos of the Tour, narrated by Liggett. Professionally edited and designed for avid cyclists, the WCP videos became hot commodities. ESPN gradually increased their coverage of the Tour.

Recently, the Outdoor Life Network (OLN) has found great success with wall-to-wall Tour de France coverage. The tour is broadcast live for three hours every weekday morning, repeated a few times in the afternoon, condensed for a prime-time show in the evening, and then the original feed is replayed late at night. More than 300 hours' coverage is broadcast over three weeks, fueled by the fact that the Tour has brought OLN its highest ratings ever. As a result of these ratings, they have a few commentary crews explaining the race, and multiple segments in their prime-time broadcast. They even supplement the television broadcasts with a website. CBS has returned to the scene with some weekend coverage in their highly successful highlight format, which, like its predecessor in the 1980s, is an Emmy-winning production.

OLN made a move reminiscent of the Tour founders by signing on as a sponsor of the U.S. Postal Service team in 2004. Their savvy move was trumped by Discovery Channel when they took over title sponsorship of the team from 2005 through 2008. Now Discovery has Lance Armstrong as a spokesman, and is not only featuring him as talent in their current lineup of shows, but also as the subject of cycling-oriented shows. As Armstrong is a part-owner of his team and has a separate contract with Discovery as well, expect him to be promoting cycling for some time to come.

All the News That's Fit to Print

Thanks to Greg and Lance, the Tour is now covered in many major newspapers across the United States. It's gratifying for cyclists and enthusiasts to see that the *New York Times* cover with Armstrong winning a stage in 2004 is one the *Times* uses in their ads for the paper. Cycling will probably come and go from many newspapers depending on how sports editors gauge their readership's interest in cycling; this will probably ebb and flow along with American success at the Tour. But it will be hard for the race to disappear, as a number of people have become fans not so much of Americans riding well, but of the Tour itself.

One place where Tour coverage will stay for a while is *USA Today*. The paper has covered the Tour since 1982, and when interest is high, fellow Gannett papers syndicate the stories. *USA Today*'s current Tour correspondent, Sal Ruibal, is an active bike racer and has been covering the race for them since 1995. Ruibal says of their coverage, "During the Tour we have something every day, but I prefer to write big-picture stories that explain what's coming up, rather than gamers on the previous day's stage. By the time a U.S. reader gets the paper, that day's stage has already begun. Our style is to tell the reader what is going to happen that day, rather than rehashing what they've already read on cyclingnews.com or seen on ESPN or OLN." If there's no room, the story ends up online only.

Ruibal thinks interest in the Tour has grown to be pretty high. "Out of that potential audience of five million (who look at the paper), perhaps a million will read something about the Tour. If it is a page 1A cover, maybe three million will read some of it. A Sports 1C cover may get a couple of million pairs of eyes. Other non-Tour cycling stories, especially if they're buried inside the Sports section, may only get a hundred thousand or so. I like to think of that audience in terms of 'Woodstocks': 500,000 readers equals one Woodstock. So a cover story could be a '4 Woodstock' piece and an inside story is just a really big Grateful Dead concert."

The Tour on the Web

And for some, web coverage of the Tour is even better than television or newspapers. In 1995, ASO made a home for itself on the Internet and created a website for the Tour. For several years the organization has been posting live reports of the races online . . . turning a computer into a fancy teletype machine that makes it easy for office workers to follow the race silently from their desks. Each single report can be short, "4:56 P.M.—Azevedo is blown." But the updates come faster toward the end of the stage and convey an immediacy to the race, possibly similar to listening to the radio. People sometimes find themselves madly hitting the "reload" key on their browser as the race goes through the final kilometers. Velonews.com's live reports are on a page that reloads automatically, and it seems too slow as people get on and read the final kilometers.

A number of websites run live reports. The two most popular sites in the Anglophone world seem to be velonews.com and cyclingnews.com. Both run Tour extravaganzas on their sites. Live reports, recaps, diaries, pictures, analyses, tech reports, everything they can throw at readers. Bicycling.com and several bike news–oriented websites post several daily reports apiece. Bike companies have also gotten into the act, with people on the ground in France commenting on either the company's sponsored riders or the use of the product, or both. Cycling teams also have websites. Online retailers have gotten into the act, creating contests based on the

Tour. There are even Tour fantasy leagues. In addition, many, many pictures are posted, both by professional photographers and by amateurs. Graham Watson, one of the most prominent photographers in the Anglophone world, puts up several shots daily at grahamwatson.com.

Some devoted fans take it all in. A question might be raised: "Do they have lives?" Some read the web at work and then watch at night, while others "save" themselves by watching the Tour at night, then checking out the websites. But not everyone has cable, or television, or web access. People take in what they can. And they'll stop this bad habit, once the Tour is over. Really. But they're probably experiencing Tour fatigue by this point anyway.

With the explosion of media options, there can only be more choices in the offing. In 2005, OLN decided not to run the Italian feed from the Giro d'Italia on their channel. While this infuriated many viewers, OLN came up with a new option. For a small fee, people could stream the last few hours of a stage on the web, and they could watch it whenever and wherever they wanted: from work, from home, at an Internet café, whatever. The people who want start-to-finish cycling coverage every day might even be able to get it in the foreseeable future.

Experiencing the Action Firsthand

At one time, many foreigners wanting to see the Tour had to be strong cyclists as well as intrepid and smart, because spectators would actually follow the Tour on their bicycles. Information on where the Tour went was hard to find, and getting details necessitated letters and calls to France. While this was a time-honored method—

many well-known British journalists and photographers got their starts bike touring ahead of the race—it was particularly difficult to both plan and ride. Still, some do this even today, if only for several days.

While a few Americans were riding around France following the Tour, the bicycle travel business was becoming more established. First largely limited to people hauling their own gear, companies started specializing in transporting people's gear from hotel to hotel and allowing them to ride without being encumbered by bags, tents, cookware, etc. Generally, the focus of these companies was not the bike riding, but the places visited and the hotels stayed. The rides were usually short and unchallenging for fit cyclists, but sufficient for those who just wanted to be out in the French countryside.

At some point, probably in the early 1990s, someone got the bright idea of marrying longer rides over challenging terrain with the luxury of a support van and nice hotels. It was a smart concept. Plenty of American cyclists want to ride the famed cols of the Tour and stand on the road and watch the Tour pass, but didn't have the information or wherewithal to put together a trip for themselves.

At least twenty companies in the United States currently offer Tour travel packages, with several others based in Canada, England, and elsewhere. They go to different places, offer different riding and viewing options, and are in different price ranges. Some specialize in luxury, while others focus on riding. A number have a former Tour racer on staff to offer his insights both for racing and riding. They also can help bring their trippers close to the racers right before or after the stage, as they probably have raced with many of the current generation of team directors.

Alex Stieda might be the first ex-professional to get involved in the Tour travel business—a nice business for the first North American yellow jersey winner. Stieda rode in only one Tour, but has now witnessed several, both as an employee of a Tour business and as a guy who runs the business himself. Other North American pros who have done the Tour travel circuit include Frankie Andreu, Chris Carmichael, Steve Bauer, and Marty Jemison. Expect more ex-pros to get into the business in the near future.

Stieda says he wants to transmit his passion for cycling to his trippers. "TV doesn't show the severity of the climbs very well. We make sure people get to ride a full length out of category climb. 'Feel of the road' is my byline. I do some skill-development issues as well. Many enthusiasts are scared, so I get them to get a better feel for control downhill, and the camaraderie of doing it with a group." If someone can't do all of the ride, they're transported farther down the road, so they do a shorter ride and still climb the mountain or finish with the group.

Stieda limits the number of hotels. Transferring hotels every night can make the vacation grueling, kind of like racing the Tour, so he tries to design the trip so each hotel is home base for three nights.

Peter Easton found the transfers bothersome as well. He started as a participant on such trips, but didn't like them. Easton decided to make his own trips to cater to the kind of cyclist he is. His company, Velo Classics, tries to offer serious riding with great places to stay. "It's not about how fast you can ride, but people can understand that there's a lot of endurance involved: four to five days of riding four or five hours a day, climbs of ten to twenty kilometers, or traveling race to race in the spring classics. But we also round the trips out with various cultural scenarios with restaurants, cities, etc., that have resonance for that region. A chef, a history, adds quality to that region." For the Tour, his trips are based out of a single hotel. The groups ride many of the climbs days ahead of the race, and then make day trips out of seeing some stages. He's been doing it for five years, and seems to have found his niche.

Interestingly, the Trek bicycle company decided to get involved in the travel business. Trek Travel offers seven different Tour trips at two different activity levels, "easy" and "avid." One trip even gets you some interaction with Trek-sponsored Discovery Channel team riders. The accommodations and access come at a price, upwards of $6,000 for the six-day trip with all the bells and whistles.

On the lower end of the price spectrum are the British Graham Baxter Tours. Here, the cost is closer to $100 a day, with a larger group and less individual attention. Still, there is as much riding as one wants, and the trip leaders have done it before, so they can find the good vantage points.

And there will always be people designing and implementing their own trips to the Tour. Since the route is announced several months ahead of the race, anyone with a sense of adventure can make her own trip to France. Some are so bold as to go over with nothing but a map of the race and a train map, winging it the whole way. Others plan ahead, reserving a car, hotel rooms, and planning rides as well as days of spectating.

Whether you're going to the Tour for the riding, the viewing, or both, every day on the Tour is an adventure. In the mountains, the roads close pretty early, three to four hours ahead of the race, so if one is considering driving up a mountain, it's crucial to get in position not only before the road closes, but before the other spots are taken up by like-minded people.

On the mountains, there will be people who go up early to camp out—some in camper vans, who might have staked out their spot days ahead of the race—others pitching tents. The early birds are often the people who draw flags and paint names and slogans on the road itself. The smart ones bring some kind of ground cover so the people driving/riding/walking up while the paint is wet don't streak the message. There will be plenty of cyclists taking advantage of the closed roads to ride up through the throngs. Many have packed what would be considered in America to be a high-end meal—table, chairs, multi-course meal, lots of wine.

Groups are initially distinct, starting with the group they got to the mountain with and those who speak the same language. It's not just the French who enjoy the Tour, but also the Dutch, Belgians, Germans, Italians, Spaniards, Swiss—essentially, a cross-section of all Europe descends on the road and has a day of doing nothing but eating, hanging out, and watching the race.

Some groups have their own identity. Maybe it is a travel group, a rider's fan club, or a group of Basques, but people will often wear something indicative of their group. Both the Basques and the Dutch are known to wear orange, but the Dutch seem to be bigger on face-painting. People will be dressed in team colors as well, though in the high mountains, it is always wise to be prepared with cold-weather gear and rainwear. Flags will be hoisted on poles and attached to cliffsides. Ostensibly, these flourishes are for the racers' benefit, but the real reason is *tifosi* pride.

Patrick Brady, editor of *Asphalt* magazine and a veteran of several spectating Tours, finds that the energy of the crowd slowly picks up. "The excitement ticks up by notches. When the *gendarmes* ride by, they start to notice. Then when the first pre-vehicles come by ten minutes later, another thrill. There's a fair amount of cheering when all the promotional vehicles pass through, and then there's a real lull. And then things really pick up when you hear the helicopter." Many have been listening to the radio or watching a portable television, and know where the race is. Those without have been trying to listen, watch, or ask questions to see what they can find out. The highest climbs are above the treeline, so it's often possible to see the race making its way up the mountain.

And then it's time for the race to pass. The leader or leaders come by to a huge cheer, but there are still more than a hundred racers behind. According to Easton, "On the Forclaz (in 2004), the race took fifteen minutes to pass through. It can be even longer. You'll get the first group, the chase, some guys who have fallen off the chase, the *grupetto*, guys who have fallen off. The guys who are about to pack it in . . . if it's the fourth or fifth group, people will cheer [more] for encouragement than for fanaticism. It's the crowd telling the riders they're supported."

The racers who look terrible and seem to be falling apart might get pushed by the fans. Sometimes drink gets passed up or water poured overhead. They might look terrible, but they're still climbing faster than most people can when they're fresh. It's their job to finish, but it's also a point of pride, and a character-building, fitness-growing enterprise.

After it's all gone, after the last rider has passed, and the broom wagon has gone by, the party doesn't need to end. If one has a bus or camper, it could take a few hours to get off the mountain. It is here when the bike again seems like a good idea. Because of the timing, in the midst of a stage, plenty of people are happy staying on the mountain, following the progress by radio or TV, making friends and excitedly anticipating the finish.

For many of the spectators, packing up means driving up a mountain on the next stage's itinerary, finding a good spot, and camping out. The next day, they'll repeat the previous.

For those who leave, there's always next year. Maybe there will be the opportunity to go to other stages, a mountain range, or the finish in Paris.

GLOSSARY

Abandon—Leave the Tour without being eliminated or disqualified. Tour riders don't quit; they are either sick or injured and can't go on.

All 'rounder—A rider who can do everything well, but isn't dominant in any single aspect of racing.

Alps—One of the two major mountain ranges in France. These mountains are on the eastern border alongside Switzerland and Italy. Every year, the Tour goes through the Alps.

Arrivée—Finish line.

Attack, Attacking—A sudden increase in effort and speed by a single rider or a group of riders. This is how breakaways usually start.

Autobus—*See "Grupetto."*

Best young rider—The person leading the competition for the white jersey, or *maillot blanc*. Sometimes the term *neophyte* is used, as the rider might not have ridden the Tour before. He has to be less than twenty-five years old. The competition is decided on time, just like the competition for the yellow jersey.

Block, Blocking—Impeding the progress of others, sometimes by deliberately riding slowly. A tactic usually employed to help further or preserve a breakaway's lead.

Blow up—What happens when someone is going too hard, too long. Suddenly, the rider can't ride nearly as hard. He looks like his engine has blown.

Bonk, Bonking—In running, this is "hitting the wall." This is what happens when one runs out of energy, usually meaning a total emptying of one's stored glucose. The result is a sudden, dramatic decrease in effort.

Breakaway—A single rider or group of riders getting away from the massive field of riders. This is how many like to win races.

Breaking away—The act of starting a breakaway, usually by attacking.

Bridge, Bridging—Short for "bridging a gap." This usually means attacking the field solo or with a small group to catch a breakaway.

Broom wagon—The last vehicle in the caravan, traditionally a minibus with an upside-down broom literally lashed to the front. It is where riders go when they abandon out of the Tour. They're getting "swept" off the course. Once in, they can't finish the day or the race.

Burning matches—A match lights bright, like an explosion. There are limited matches in any matchbox. For racers, the metaphor is that they are lighting a match each time they attack or accelerate hard. At a certain point, they will run out of matches.

Cadence—The rate at which one's legs pedal a revolution of the crankset. Referred to in units known as revolutions per minute (rpm). Ninety rpm is considered ideal; below 80 is often considered "mashing" and above 100 rpm is often considered "spinning."

Caravan—The group of vehicles that follows behind the racers. It is composed of cars and motorcycles filled with race officials, *gendarmes*, team support staff, and medical personnel.

Caravane Publicitaire—"The publicity caravan." It is a giant procession of cars, vans, and motorcycles preceding the race that functions as a moving advertisement for the race sponsors.

Champs-Elysées—"Elysian Fields," the most famous avenue in

Paris. Every year, the final stage of the Tour finishes on the Champs-Elysées.

Chase, Chasing—The effort to catch someone who has ridden up the road, usually in a breakaway, though one can chase to catch the field after a flat or crash.

Circuit race—A stage or race comprised of multiple laps around a long circuit of roads.

Classic—A long, tough, one-day race. Classics are considered the toughest cohort of one-day races on the professional calendar, as well as monuments of cycling. They're usually over 150 miles in length. Some of the classics have been in existence for over 100 years. Classic races include Milan-San Remo, Tour of Flanders, Liege–Bastogne Liege, and Paris-Roubaix.

Classment General, Classment—*See "General classification."*

Climber—Someone whose specialty is going uphill. Typically, these riders appear to be smaller and leaner than the average racer.

Climber's jersey—*See "Maillot blanc et rouge."*

Cobbles—Short for cobblestone roads. The ancient method for paving, which is why they're sometimes referred to as pave. They last forever, and Europe has plenty of roads paved by this method from antiquity. Some cobbles are smooth and easy to ride, but many are rough and hard to ride.

Col—A mountain.

Commissaire—Race official. Commissaires enforce the rules for the UCI.

Complete rider—The kind of rider who is supposed to win the Tour. He can climb, time trial, sprint, and ride the flats well, and never have a bad day.

Contre le montre—"Against the watch." *See "time trial."*

Cornering—Turning a bike while riding it.

Crash—Racers don't fall. They crash.

Criterium—In the United States, a race comprised of multiple laps of a short circuit, usually a mile in length or less. In Europe, criterium can be used as a description of almost any length race.

Crosswind—Wind blowing from the left or right side, as opposed to blowing from the front (headwind) or rear (tailwind).

Cyclocross—A bicycle racing discipline that's kind of like steeplechase on a bicycle. 'Cross, as it is known to fans, takes place in the fall and winter months.

Départ—Start line.

Derailleur—Device that shifts gears on a bike. Most bikes have both front and rear derailleurs, front shifts chainrings, rear shifts cogs. So named because it derails the chain.

Directeur Sportif—"Sports director." This is the manager of the team, the guy who is in charge of everything that goes on for his team.

Division one—Sometimes written as DI or TTI (trade team one). A recently abandoned term, though it might still be used by some. The updated term is UCI Pro Team. There are three divisions of professional cycling teams in the world. The highest are ranked in division one. Teams in the top division are automatically selected for the Tour.

Dnf—Did not finish.

Dns—Did not start.

Domestique—Worker, taken from the French for servant. Racer who rides in support of a team leader, sacrificing his own chances so the leader can do well.

Dope, Doping—Illegal performance-enhancing substances. These substances, usually chemical in nature, are banned by the UCI for competitive cyclists to use in or out of competition, but are not necessarily illegal for noncompetitors to use. There is a long list of banned substances, some of which are hard to find, while others appear in over-the-counter medication and supplements. The well-known banned substances include: anabolic steroids, epo (erythropoietin), and human growth hormone.

Draft, Drafting—An essential concept to mass-start bicycle racing. A draft is the pocket of wind that a cyclist creates by riding. The faster the rider goes, the bigger the draft gets. Drafting is tucking behind another rider or a group of riders to save energy. The faster one goes, the more one can save energy by utilizing this technique. Riding solo at 25 mph is roughly equivalent to riding over 30 mph behind someone. The effect is magnified as the pack gets larger.

Drive, Driver, Driving—The person who is the strongest or in charge of a group. Up front, someone drives a breakaway. At the back, someone drives the *grupetto*.

Drop, Dropping, Dropped—To drop someone is to leave them behind. Getting dropped is to be left behind. Sometimes it's because the pace is too fast; sometimes it's because the rider getting dropped is too weak to stay with the group or rider ahead of him.

Échappée—Escape.

Échappée royale—"Escape of the leaders." When the best riders in the race break away together.

Echelon—A riding formation for moving quickly through crosswinds. The riders splay out in a diagonal across the road, much like the way migrating birds fly together.

En masse—The field riding together. Usually mentioned when the field is all together, riding to the finish.

False flat—A road that appears flat but is really a slight incline.

Feed Zone—A small stretch of road in the middle of a stage where a rider can pick up food from a helper standing at the side of the road. If the stage is more than a certain length, there will be two feed zones.

Field—"Pack" or *peloton*. All the competitors in a race comprise the field.

Field sprint—A large group of riders sprinting together for a finish line.

Flat, the—Flat roads. No elevation gained or lost.

Flat tire—Air leaves the tire through a cut or hole of some sort. A flat tire can't be ridden on for long, and the bicycle is disabled until the flat tire is replaced with another wheel.

Flick, Flicked, Flicking—Removing another rider from a group by strength or cunning. "He flicked me" is common usage. The result is lost position and often lost time. The term is usually negative.

Flame rouge—"Red flame." A red flag, flickering in the wind like a flame, is flown to mark the start of the final kilometer of a stage or race.

French—The official language of bicycle racing. Thanks to location and the Tour, the nation is at the epicenter of European pro bike racing.

Full gas—Racing full-throttle, all-out.

Gear, Gearing—Most racing bicycles have eighteen or twenty gears, or speeds on them. That usually means they have two chainrings on the right crankarm and nine or ten sprockets on the rear cassette. Racers shift gears to maintain optimum cadence at all times.

Gendarme—Policeman.

General classification—The standings of the Tour based on time. The leader of the race has the lowest overall elapsed time. Many riders refer to it as the *classement* for the French version of the same name.

Giro d'Italia—Tour of Italy. Italy's grand tour.

Grand tour—A three-week-long stage race. There are three of them every year: the Tour, the Giro d'Italia, and the Vuelta a España.

Green jersey—*Maillot vert*. The jersey worn by the rider leading the points standings in the race. Points are totaled every day and are cumulative. The green jersey, like the yellow jersey, can change every day.

Gregario—*See "Domestique."*

Grimpeur—"Climber."

Grupetto—A group of racers who aren't racing to win on a particular stage, but are riding merely to finish within the time cut. Also known as "autobus."

Gruppo compatto—The field, or group, riding wide across the road, compacting them in length. This is what happens when the pace is easy.

Hammering—Riding hard. When the racing suddenly gets painfully fast, someone has "dropped the hammer."

Headbanger—Someone who specializes in breakaways that last most of a stage.

Hill climb—A race that goes up a hill.

Hook—A maneuver in which the lead rider swerves his bike to prevent another rider from passing. Sometimes seen in sprint finishes. If seen and judged dangerous by officials, a hook can lead to relegation.

Hors Category (HC)—"Beyond category." Climbs are categorized at the Tour. The hardest are HC.

Hot spot—*See "Intermediate Sprint."*

Hour Record—The farthest anyone has been able to travel on a track bicycle on a velodrome in an hour. In 1893, Henri Desgrange set the hour record at 35.325 km. Several Tour champions have pushed the record further. Ondrej Sosenka, a racer from the Czech Republic, set the latest hour record at the Moscow Velodrome on July 19, 2005. He traveled 49.7 km in an hour, and holds the current record.

Intermediate Sprint—A finish line often put in a town somewhere in the middle of a stage. This race within a race helps keep the race from slowing down and it gives townsfolk a reason to come out and watch the race pass through their town. Intermediate sprints are always worth money and points; sometimes they're also worth time bonuses.

Jersey—Cycling top. Usually has a zippered collar, three pockets in the back, is form-fitting, and designed to be comfortable in the riding position.

Jour Sans—"A day without." The connotation is a day without pleasure. In the Tour, a *jour sans* is the day when a top rider is feeling terrible and rides poorly. Supposedly, the winner of the Tour never has such a day during the race.

Jump—A synonym of attack.

Kick—A synonym of sprint.

Kilometer—Equivalent to 0.625 mile. International bicycle racing is officially measured in kilometers. For those stuck on the English system, here are some approximates: 10 kph = 6 mph; 20 = 12.5 mph; 30 = 19; 40 = 25; 50 = 31; 60 = 37; 70 = 43; 100 = 62.5.

King of the Mountains (KoM)—The wearer of the polka-dot jersey. A common competition in many stage races and some road races.

Kit—A British term for uniform.

Lanterne rouge—"Red Lantern." The last-placed rider of the race. He's given a red lantern, symbolic of the back of a train.

Laughing Group—*See "Grupetto."*

Le Tête de la Course—"The Head of the Race," or the front.

Lead out—Setting someone up for sprint or attack. The lead out person, intentionally or accidentally, helps set up the rider behind him to give a burst of speed. The lead out man is the person who helps set up a sprinter for his final two-hundred-meter burst to the finish line.

Maillot à pois—*See Maillot blanc et rouge.*

Maillot blanc—The white jersey worn by the leader of the Best Young Rider competition.

Maillot blanc et rouge—A white jersey with red polka dots, worn by the leader of the mountain climber competition.

Maillot jaune—The yellow jersey, worn by the leader of the race, the person with the lowest cumulative time on General Classification. To minimize confusion, no other team is allowed to wear jerseys with yellow as the dominant color.

Maillot vert—The green jersey, worn by the leader of the points competition.

Mass-Start—When everyone in a race starts at the same time together. The winner of a mass-start race is the first person over the finish line. Drafting is one of the most important strategic techniques in this sort of race.

Mechanical—A general term for any mechanical mishap that occurs to a bicycle.

Most combative—Sometimes written as "combativity." A daily award given to the most aggressive racer of a given day, decided by journalists. There is also a most aggressive rider award for the Tour.

Mountain goat—Someone who can climb hills well. Mountain goats seem to just scoot uphill, which is similar to how these riders move uphill.

Mountains competition, Mountains classification—Points awarded to the first riders over a categorized climb during a stage.

Musette bag—A small cloth bag with a long shoulder loop. These are used by *soigneurs* at feed zones to hand food and drink up to racers whizzing by. The *soigneur* holds out the goody-filled bag and the racers grab the bags as they race by, put the strap over their shoulder, fill their pockets and cages, and toss the bag.

National champion—A person who has won his nation's one-day national championship event. The national champion gets to wear a jersey in the colors of his nation's flag for the year following his victory. He is then entitled to wear special stripes on his sleeves denoting the prior achievement.

Neo-Pro—Short for neophyte professional. A first-year pro, a rookie.

Neutral support—This is a team support car for every rider in the race. Any racer can go to them and get a spare wheel or bike.

No hoper—Someone who has no hope of winning a race.

Off the back (OTB)—OTB. Someone or a group who is behind the field.

Off the front—Someone or a group who is ahead of the field, usually *le tete en course*.

On the boil—The race is heating up almost to the boiling point.

On the rivet—Similar to "on the boil." The race is really fast. You can tell because the riders are moving themselves forward on their saddles, almost sitting on the nose, where a saddle rivet used to be.

Opportunist—Someone who sees an opportunity to do well and takes advantage of it, even if it's a long shot.

Paceline—A group of riders riding in a coordinated fashion so each takes a turn at the front to break the wind for everyone behind him.

Pack—A large group of riders together in a big bunch.

Palmares—A commonly used synonym for "results."

Parade—A nonrace procession usually for the first few kilometers of every stage.

Patron—A racer in the pack who is imbued with the authority to control the race. Often this rider is a multi-Tour winner.

Pavé—A synonym for cobblestone roads.

Peloton—*See "Pack."*

Piano—An easy pace.

Points competition, Points classification—A second competition within the Tour. This competition rewards consistency and the ability to sprint several times a day.

Polka-dot jersey—*See "Maillot blanc et rouge."*

Prime—Pronounced "preem." A prize given sometime before the finish of a stage.

Prologue—A short time trial positioned at the first day of racing. Usually only a few kilometers in length, they are largely for the benefit of spectators, and to award someone the yellow jersey in advance of the first day of racing.

Pro Tour—The race calendar of the most important races; only the strongest teams receive an automatic invitation to these races.

Pull—Leading a paceline. The idea is that the first rider is pulling the group through the wind. The person pulling is doing more work than anyone behind him.

Pull off—When the leader of a paceline moves to the side to drift back and take a rest.

Pull through—After the leader pulls off, the second rider in the line pedals past the first into the lead.

Pursuit—Both the act of chasing and a kind of race on the track where one chases another rider for several kilometers.

Push—Sometimes, rider and fans exhort someone to ride well. Other times, there is literally pushing. Technically, pushing by riders, fans, and team personnel is against the rules, but there are times when it is tolerated. Can be seen when stragglers are climbing up a long mountain at the end of a long day.

Pyrenees—The mountain range in southern France that borders Spain.

Race of Truth—A colorful synonym for time trial. A time trial is the race of truth because there is no place to hide.

Relegation—A punishment meted out in dropping someone's placing. This is most commonly seen as the result of illegal maneuvers during a sprint finish. Sometimes someone who places well will have done so with an illegal hook, push, or shove. The finisher will see his placing reduced from being at or near the front to at or near the back. An extreme example is going from first to 189th because of that infraction.

Roleur—"Roller." Someone who is a good time trialist.

Semi-classic—A step down from a *Classic*. A semi-classic is usually shorter in length and has a less competitive field than a classic; it also usually has less prize money and a slightly weaker field of racers.

Sprint—A short, intense effort. Any all-out effort from zero to five hundred meters is considered a sprint.

Switchback—A point on a road where it makes a sharp turn, close to 180 degrees. Often found on mountains.

Team time trial (TTT)—Similar to a time trial, only the entire team starts together and the time is taken on the fifth rider to cross the finish line.

Time penalty—Race officials add some time, to penalize the rider for certain kinds of rule breaking. Usually the penalties are to make amends for an illegal advantage some rider took.

Time trial (TT)—Every rider starts by himself, has to ride by himself, and the winner is the person who rides the fastest time. Called the "race of truth" because no rider can work with another rider or hide from the wind.

Toast—A.k.a. "cooked," or "finished." When someone is too tired to maintain a pace, they're toasted.

Tour de France—*Le grand boucle*, the race of races. The World Series of cycling.

Track racing—A discipline of cycling that only takes place on velodromes. The events are generally short and fast.

UCI—Union Cycliste Internationale (International Cycling Union), the international governing body of bicycle racing.

White jersey—*See "Maillot Blanc."*

Wildcard selection—A team chosen for participation by the promoter. Up to four teams every year can get such an invite. These teams aren't amongst the automatic invites.

World Champion—The person who has won the one-day world championship in a particular discipline. The world champion wears a jersey with rainbow stripes signifying his accomplishment for the year following his victory. After that year, the rider is allowed to wear the rainbow stripes on his sleeves.

World Cup—A series of mostly European classics that take place throughout the season. Succeeded in 2005 by The Pro Tour.

Velodrome—A bicycle track. These are usually between 200 and 333.33 meters long and are banked in the turns.

Victory—Any win is a victory. It can be for hot-spot sprints, a stage victory, a victory in a jersey competition, or overall victory in the race.

Ville Départ—Temporary town set up for the racers and support staff by the start line of a stage.

Voiture balai—*See "Broom wagon."*

Yellow jersey—*See "Maillot Jaune."*

Appendix A

AMERICANS AT THE TOUR

The American invasion of the Tour began in 1981. Jonathan "Jacques" Boyer rode as a *domestique* on Bernard Hinault's Renault-Elf-Gitane team, and helped Hinault to his third Tour victory. Since this auspicious start, Americans in particular, and non-Europeans in general, have had an amazingly successful run at the Tour.

Thanks to these hardy souls, Americans riding the Tour might not cause too much notice, as they've been doing well enough for long enough that they belong.

North American Rider Participation in the Tour de France

AMERICANS AT THE TOUR

Participation through 2005

1981 **32.** Jonathan Boyer, Renault-Elf-Gitane

1982 **23.** Jonathan Boyer, Sem

1983 **12.** Jonathan Boyer, Sem

1984 **3.** Greg LeMond, Renault-Elf-Gitane; 2nd in white jersey competition

1985 **2.** Greg LeMond, La Vie Claire; winner, combination jersey
74. Doug Shapiro, Kwantum
Stage winner: Greg LeMond, Limoges–Lac de Vassiviere (TT)

1986 **1.** Greg LeMond, La Vie Claire
4. Andy Hampsten, La Vie Claire, winner, white jersey competition
63. Bob Roll, 7-Eleven
80. Jeff Pierce, 7-Eleven
96. Ron Kiefel, 7-Eleven
DNF. Chris Carmichael, Alexi Grewal, Eric Heiden, Davis Phinney, Doug Shapiro, all 7-Eleven
Stage winners: Greg LeMond, Pau–Superbagneres; Davis Phinney, Levallois–Lievin

1987 **16.** Andy Hampsten, 7-Eleven
82. Ron Kiefel, 7-Eleven
88. Jeff Pierce, 7-Eleven
98. Jonathan Boyer, 7-Eleven
DNF. Jeff Bradley, Davis Phinney, Bob Roll, all 7-Eleven
Stage winners: Jeff Pierce, Creteil–Paris; Davis Phinney, Brive–Bordeaux

1988 **15.** Andy Hampsten, 7-Eleven
69. Ron Kiefel, 7-Eleven
105. Davis Phinney, 7-Eleven, second in points competition
135. Andy Bishop, PDM
DNF. Roy Knickman, Jeff Pierce, both 7-Eleven

1989 **1.** Greg LeMond, ADR
22. Andy Hampsten, 7-Eleven
73. Ron Kiefel, 7-Eleven
86. Jeff Pierce, 7-Eleven
DNF. Roy Knickman, 7-Eleven
Stage winners: Greg LeMond, Dinard–Rennes (TT); Villard-de-Lans–Aix-les-Bains; Versailles–Paris (TT)

1990 **1.** Greg LeMond, Z
11. Andy Hampsten, 7-Eleven
83. Ron Kiefel, 7-Eleven
132. Bob Roll, 7-Eleven
142. Norman Alvis, 7-Eleven
153. Davis Phinney, 7-Eleven

1991 **7.** Greg LeMond, Z
8. Andy Hampsten, Motorola
126. Andy Bishop, Motorola
138. Ron Kiefel, Motorola
DNF. Mike Carter, Motorola

1992 **4.** Andy Hampsten, Motorola
110. Frankie Andreu, Motorola
DNF. Andy Bishop, Ron Kiefel, both Motorola; Greg LeMond, Z
Stage winner: Andy Hampsten, Sestrieres–L'Alpe d'Huez

1993 **8.** Andy Hampsten, Motorola
89. Frankie Andreu, Motorola
DNF. Lance Armstrong, Motorola
Stage winner: Lance Armstrong, Chalons-sur-Marne–Verdun

1994 **89.** Frankie Andreu, Motorola
DNF. Lance Armstrong, Motorola; Greg LeMond, Gan

1995 **36.** Lance Armstrong, Motorola
82. Frankie Andreu, Motorola
Stage winner: Lance Armstrong, Montpon–Monesterol–Limoges

1996 **111.** Frankie Andreu, Motorola
DNF. Lance Armstrong, George Hincapie, both Motorola

1997 **17.** Bobby Julich, Cofidis
38. Kevin Livingston, Cofidis
69. Tyler Hamilton, U.S. Postal Service
79. Frankie Andreu, Cofidis
96. Marty Jemison, U.S. Postal Service
104. George Hincapie, U.S. Postal Service

1998 **3.** Bobby Julich, Cofidis
17. Kevin Livingston, Cofidis
48. Marty Jemison, U.S. Postal Service
51. Tyler Hamilton, U.S. Postal Service
53. George Hincapie, U.S. Postal Service
58. Frankie Andreu, U.S. Postal Service

1999 **1.** Lance Armstrong, U.S. Postal Service
13. Tyler Hamilton, U.S. Postal Service
65. Frankie Andreu, U.S. Postal Service
78. George Hincapie, U.S. Postal Service
85. Christian Vande Velde, U.S. Postal Service
DNF. Bobby Julich, Cofidis; Jonathan Vaughters, U.S. Postal Service
Stage winner: Lance Armstrong, Le Puy du Fou (TT); Metz (TT); Le Grand Bornand–Sestrieres; Futuroscope (TT)

2000 **1.** Lance Armstrong, U.S. Postal Service
25. Tyler Hamilton, U.S. Postal Service
37. Kevin Livingston, U.S. Postal Service
48. Bobby Julich, Credit Agricole
65. George Hincapie, U.S. Postal Service
86. Fred Rodriguez, Mapei
110. Frankie Andreu, U.S. Postal Service
DNF. Chann McRae, Mapei; Jonathan Vaughters, Credit Agricole
Stage winner: Lance Armstrong, Fribourg-en-Brisgau–Mulhouse (TT)

2001 **1.** Lance Armstrong, U.S. Postal Service
18. Bobby Julich, Credit Agricole
43. Kevin Livingston, Telekom
71. George Hincapie, U.S. Postal Service
94. Tyler Hamilton, U.S. Postal Service
DNF. Fred Rodriguez, Domo-Farm Frites; Christian Vande Velde, U.S. Postal Service; Jonathan Vaughters, Credit Agricole
Stage winner: Lance Armstrong, Aix les Bains–L'Alpe d'Huez; Grenoble–Chamrousse (TT); Foix–Saint Lary Soulan; Montlucon–Saint Amand Montrond (TT); Verdun-Bar Les Duc (TTT) Credit Agricole, containing Bobby Julich and Jonathan Vaughters

2002 **1.** Lance Armstrong, U.S. Postal Service
8. Levi Leipheimer, Rabobank

15. Tyler Hamilton, CSC
37. Bobby Julich, Telekom
56. Kevin Livingston, Telekom
61. Floyd Landis, U.S. Postal Service
59. George Hincapie, U.S. Postal Service
DNF. Fred Rodriguez, Domo-Farm Frites; Jonathan Vaughters, Credit Agricole
Stage winner: Lance Armstrong, Luxembourg–Luxembourg; Pau–La Mongie; Lannemezan–Plateau de Beille; Regnie Durette–Macon

2003 **1.** Lance Armstrong, U.S. Postal Service
4. Tyler Hamilton, CSC
47. George Hincapie, U.S. Postal Service
77. Floyd Landis, U.S. Postal Service
DNF. Levi Leipheimer, Rabobank; Fred Rodriguez, Vini Caldirola-Sidermec
Stage winners: Tyler Hamilton, Pau–Bayonne; Lance Armstrong, Bagneres de Bigorre–Luz-Ardiden; Joinville–St. Dizier (TTT)

2004 **1.** Lance Armstrong, U.S. Postal Service
9. Levi Leipheimer, Rabobank
23. Floyd Landis, U.S. Postal Service
33. George Hincapie, U.S. Postal Service
40. Bobby Julich, CSC
56. Christian Vande Velde, Liberty Seguros
DNF. Tyler Hamilton, Phonak
Stage winner: Lance Armstrong, Lannemezan–Plateau de Beille; Valreas–Villard-de-Lans; Bourg-d'Oisans–L'Alpe d'Huez; Bourg-d'Oisans–Le Grand Bornand; Besancon–Besancon (TT); Cambrai–Arras (TTT)

2005 **1.** Lance Armstrong, Discovery Channel Pro Cycling Team
6. Levi Leipheimer, Gerolsteiner
9. Floyd Landis, Phonak
14. George Hincapie, Discovery Channel Pro Cycling Team
17. Bobby Julich, CSC
33. Christopher Horner, Saunier Duval
132. Fred Rodriguez, Davitamon-Lotto
139. Guido Trenti, Quick Step-Innergetic
DNF. David Zabriskie, CSC (wore yellow jersey for three stages)
Stage winners: Lance Armstrong, Saint-Etienne–Saint-

Etienne; George Hincapie, Lézat-sur-Leze–Saint-Lary-Soulan; David Zabriskie, Fromentine–Noirmoutier en l'ile.

AMERICAN TEAMS

1986–1990	7-Eleven
1991–1996	Motorola
1997–2004	U.S. Postal Service
2005–	Discovery Channel Pro Cycling

OTHER NORTH AMERICAN RIDERS AT THE TOUR

1985 **10.** Steve Bauer (Can.), La Vie Claire, wore white jersey

1986 **23.** Steve Bauer (Can.), La Vie Claire
114. Raul Alcala (Mex.), 7-Eleven
120. Alex Stieda (Can.), 7-Eleven, wore yellow jersey

1987 **9.** Raul Alcala (Mex.), 7-Eleven, wore white and polka-dot jerseys
74. Steve Bauer (Can.), La Vie Claire

1988 **4.** Steve Bauer (Can.), Weinmann-La Suisse, won stage, wore yellow jersey
20. Raul Alcala (Mex.), 7-Eleven

1989 **8.** Raul Alcala (Mex.), PDM, won stage
15. Steve Bauer (Can.), Helvetia-La Suisse

1990 **8.** Raul Alcala (Mex.), PDM, won stage
27. Steve Bauer (Can.), 7-Eleven, wore yellow jersey

1991 **98.** Steve Bauer (Can.), Motorola
DNF. Raul Alcala (Mex.), PDM

1992 **21.** Raul Alcala (Mex.), Word Perfect
DNF. Steve Bauer (Can.), Motorola

1993 **27.** Raul Alcala (Mex.), Word Perfect
101. Steve Bauer (Can.), Motorola

1994 **48.** Miguel Arroyo (Mex.), Chazal
70. Raul Alcala (Mex.), Word Perfect
DNF. Steve Bauer (Can.), Motorola

1995 **61.** Miguel Arroyo (Mex.), Chazal
101. Steve Bauer (Can.), Motorola

1997 **76.** Miguel Arroyo (Mex.), Big Mat
DNF. Gordon Fraser (Can.), Mutuelle Seine et Marne

Appendix B

TOUR PODIUMS

Winners, Podiums, and Jerseys from Tours Past

KEY TO ABBREVIATIONS:

BYR:	Best Young Rider
TEAM:	Team award
POINTS:	Points winner
KoM:	King of the Mountain

TOUR DE FRANCE WINNERS

YEAR	RIDERS ON THE PODIUM	TIME	AVG SPD	STAGES	KMS
1903	**1.** Maurice Garin (Fra)	94.33.14	25.6	6	2,428
	2. Lucien Pothier (Fra)	02.59.02			
	3. Fernand Augereau (Fra)	04.29.24			
	TEAM La Francaise Dunlop				
	Starters 60				
	Finishers 21				
1904	**1.** Henri Cornet (Fra)	96.05.00	24.3	6	2,388
	2. Jean-Baptiste Dortignacq (Fra)	02.16.14			
	3. Philippe Jousselin (Fra)	09.01.25			
	TEAM La Francaise Dunlop				
	Starters 88				
	Finishers 23				
1905	**1.** Louis Trousselier (Fra)	109.55.39	27.3	11	2,994
	2. Hippolyte Aucouturier (Fra)	+61 points			
	3. Jean-Baptiste Dortignacq (Fra)	+61 points			
	TEAM Peugot				
	Starters 60				
	Finishers 24				
1906	**1.** René Pottier (Fra)	185.47.26	24.5	13	4,637
	2. Georges Passerieu (Fra)	+8 points			
	3. Louis Trousselier (Fra)	+28 points			
	TEAM Peugot				
	Starters 82				
	Finishers 14				
1907	**1.** Lucien Petit-Breton (Fra)	156.22.30	28.5	14	4,488
	2. Gustave Garrigou (Fra)	+19 points			
	3. Louis Trousselier (Fra)	+27 points			
	TEAM Peugot				
	Starters 93				
	Finishers 33				
1908	**1.** Lucien Petit-Breton (Fra)	156.09.31	28.7	14	4,488
	2. François Faber (Lux)	+32 points			
	3. Georges Passerieu (Fra)	+39 points			

YEAR	RIDERS ON THE PODIUM	TIME	AVG SPD	STAGES	KMS
	TEAM Peugot				
	Starters 114				
	Finishers 36				
1909	**1.** François Faber (Lux)	**156.55.10**	**28.6**	**14**	**4,488**
	2. Gustave Garrigou (Fra)	**+20 points**			
	3. Jean Alavoine (Fra)	**+29 points**			
	TEAM Alcyon Pneus Dunlop				
	Starters 150				
	Finishers 55				
1910	**1.** Octave Lapize (Fra)	**163.52.38**	**28.7**	**15**	**4,737**
	2. François Faber (Lux)	**+4 points**			
	3. Gustave Garrigou (Fra)	**+23 points**			
	TEAM Alcyon Pneus Dunlop				
	Starters 110				
	Finishers 44				
1911	**1.** Gustave Garrigou (Fra)	**195.35.25**	**27.3**	**15**	**5,344**
	2. Paul Duboc (Fra)	**+18 points**			
	3. Émile Georget (Fra)	**+41 points**			
	TEAM Alcyon Pneus Dunlop				
	Starters 84				
	Finishers 28				
1912	**1.** Odile Defraye (Bel)	**190.34.00**	**27.9**	**15**	**5,319**
	2. Eugène Christophe (Fra)	**+59 points**			
	3. Gustave Garrigou (Fra)	**+91 points**			
	TEAM Alcyon Pneus Dunlop				
	Starters 131				
	Finishers 41				
1913	**1.** Philippe Thijs (Bel)	**197.54.00**	**27.6**	**15**	**5,388**
	2. Gustave Garrigou (Fra)	**-8.37 (?)**			
	3. Marcel Buysse (Bel)	**-3.30.55**			
	TEAM Peugot				
	Starters 140				
	Finishers 25				
1914	**1.** Philippe Thijs (Bel)	**200.28.48**	**27.0**	**15**	**5,405**
	2. Henri Pélissier (Fra)	**-0.01.50**			

YEAR	RIDERS ON THE PODIUM	TIME	AVG SPD	STAGES	KMS
	3. Jean Alavoine (Fra)	-0.36.53			
	TEAM Peugot				
	Starters 145				
	Finishers 54				
1919	**1.** Firmin Lambot (Bel)	231.07.15	25.0	15	5,560
	2. Jean Alavoine (Fra)	-01.42.45			
	3. Eugène Christophe (Fra)	-02.26.31			
	TEAM La Sportive				
	Starters 69				
	Finishers 10				
1920	**1.** Philippe Thijs (Bel)	228.36.00	24.1	15	5,519
	2. Hector Heuseghem (Bel)	-0.57.21			
	3. Firmin Lambot (Bel)	-1.39.35			
	TEAM La Sportive				
	Starters 113				
	Finishers 22				
1921	**1.** Léon Scieur (Bel)	221.50.26	24.7	15	5,484
	2. Hector Heuseghem (Bel)	-18.36			
	3. Honore Barthélémy (Fra)	-2.01.00			
	TEAM La Sportive				
	Starters 123				
	Finishers 38				
1922	**1.** Firmin Lambot (Bel)	222.08.06	24.2	15	5,372
	2. Jean Alavoine (Fra)	-41.15			
	3. Félix Sellier (Fra)	-42.02			
	TEAM Peugot-PneusLion				
	Starters 120				
	Finishers 38				
1923	**1.** Henri Pélissier (Fra)	222.15.30	24.4	15	5,386
	2. Ottavio Bottechia (Ita)	-30.41			
	3. Romain Bellenger (Fra)	-1.04.43			
	TEAM Automoto-Hutchinson				
	Starters 139				
	Finishers 48				

YEAR	RIDERS ON THE PODIUM	TIME	AVG SPD	STAGES	KMS
1924	**1.** Ottavio Bottechia (Ita)	226.18.21	24.0	15	5,427
	2. Nicolas Frantz (Lux)	-35.36			
	3. Lucien Buysse (Bel)	-1.32.13			
	TEAM Automoto-Hutchinson				
	Starters 157				
	Finishers 60				
1925	**1.** Ottavio Bottechia (Ita)	219.10.18	24.8	18	5,430
	2. Lucien Buysse (Bel)	-54.20			
	3. Bartolomeo Aimo (Ita)	-56.37			
	TEAM Automoto-Hutchinson				
	Starters 130				
	Finishers 49				
1926	**1.** Lucien Buysse (Bel)	238.44.25	24.1	17	5,745
	2. Nicolas Frantz (Lux)	-1.22.25			
	3. Bartolomeo Aimo (Ita)	-1.22.51			
	TEAM Automoto-Hutchinson				
	Starters 126				
	Finishers 41				
1927	**1.** Nicolas Frantz (Lux)	198.16.42	27.2	24	5,321
	2. Maurice De Waele (Bel)	-1.48.21			
	3. Julien Vervaecke (Bel)	-2.25.065			
	TEAM Alcyon				
	Starters 142				
	Finishers 39				
1928	**1.** Nicolas Frantz (Lux)	192.48.58	27.0	22	5,377
	2. André Leducq (Fra)	-50.07			
	3. Maurice De Waele (Bel)	-56.16			
	TEAM Alcyon				
	Starters 162				
	Finishers 41				
1929	**1.** Maurice De Waele (Bel)	186.39.15	28.3	22	5,276
	2. Guiseppe Pancera (Ita)	-44.23			
	3. Jos Demuysère (Bel)	-57.16			
	TEAM Alcyon				

YEAR	RIDERS ON THE PODIUM	TIME	AVG SPD	STAGES	KMS
	Starters 155				
	Finishers 60				
1930	**1.** André Leducq (Fra)	172.12.16	28.0	21	4,818
	2. Learco Guerra (Ita)	-14.13			
	3. Antonin Magne (Fra)	-16.03			
	TEAM France				
	Starters 100				
	Finishers 50				
1931	**1.** Antonin Magne (Fra)	177.10.03	28.8	24	5,095
	2. Jos Demuysère (Bel)	-12.56			
	3. Antonio Pesenti (Ita)	-22.51			
	TEAM Belgium				
	Starters 81				
	Finishers 35				
1932	**1.** André Leducq (Fra)	154.11.49	29.3	21	4,520
	2. Kurt Stoepel (Ger)	-24.03			
	3. Francesco Camusse (Ita)	-26.21			
	TEAM Italy				
	Starters 80				
	Finishers 57				
1933	**1.** Georges Speicher (Fra)	147.51.37	29.7	23	4,395
	2. Learco Guerra (Ita)	-4.01			
	3. Guiseppe Martano (Ita)	-5.08			
	KoM Vicente Treuba (Spa)				
	TEAM France				
	Starters 80				
	Finishers 40				
1934	**1.** Antonin Magne (Fra)	147.13.58	31.2	23	4,363
	2. Guiseppe Martano (Ita)	-27.31			
	3. Roger Lapébie (Fra)	-52.15			
	KoM René Vietto (Fra)				
	TEAM France				
	Starters 60				
	Finishers 39				

YEAR	RIDERS ON THE PODIUM	TIME	AVG SPD	STAGES	KMS
1935	**1.** Romain Maes (Bel)	141.32.00	30.6	21	4,302
	2. Ambrogio Morelli (Ita)	-17.52			
	3. Fèlicien Vervaecke (Bel)	-24.06			
	KoM Fèlicien Vervaecke (Bel)				
	TEAM Belgium				
	Starters 93				
	Finishers 46				
1936	**1.** Sylvere Maes (Bel)	142.47.32	31.1	21	4,442
	2. Antonin Magne (Fra)	-26.55			
	3. Fèlicien Vervaecke (Bel)	-27.53			
	KoM Julio Berrendero (Spa)				
	TEAM Belgium				
	Starters 90				
	Finishers 43				
1937	**1.** Roger Lapébie (Fra)	138.58.31	31.7	20	4,415
	2. Mario Vicini (Ita)	-7.17			
	3. Leo Amberg (Swi)	-26.13			
	KoM Fèlicien Vervaecke (Bel)				
	TEAM France				
	Starters 98				
	Finishers 45				
1938	**1.** Gino Bartali (Ita)	148.29.12	31.6	21	4,694
	2. Fèlicien Vervaecke (Bel)	-18.27			
	3. Victor Cosson (Fra)	-29.26			
	KoM Gino Bartali (Ita)				
	TEAM Belgium				
	Starters 96				
	Finishers 55				
1939	**1.** Sylvère Maes (Bel)	132.03.17	31.9	18	4,225
	2. René Vietto (Fra)	-30.38			
	3. Lucien Vlaeminck (Bel)	-32.08			
	KoM Sylvère Maes (Bel)				
	TEAM Belgium				
	Starters 79				
	Finishers 49				

YEAR	RIDERS ON THE PODIUM	TIME	AVG SPD	STAGES	KMS
1947	**1.** Jean Robic (Fra)	148.11.25	31.4	21	4,642
	2. Édouard Fachleitner (Fra)	-3.58			
	3. Pierre Brambilla (Ita)	-10.07			
	KoM Pierre Brambilla (Ita)				
	TEAM Italy				
	Starters 100				
	Finishers 53				
1948	**1.** Gino Bartali (Ita)	147.10.36	33.4	21	4,813
	2. Albéric "Brik" Schotte (Bel)	-26.16			
	3. Guy Lapébie (Fra)	-28.48			
	KoM Gino Bartali (Ita)				
	TEAM Belgium				
	Starters 120				
	Finishers 55				
1949	**1.** Fausto Coppi (Ita)	149.40.49	32.1	21	4,808
	2. Gino Bartali (Ita)	-10.55			
	3. Jacques Marinelli (Fra)	-25.13			
	KoM Fausto Coppi (Ita)				
	TEAM Italy				
	Starters 120				
	Finishers 55				
1950	**1.** Ferdi Kübler (Swi)	145.36.56	32.8	22	4,775
	2. Stan Ockers (Bel)	-9.30			
	3. Louison Bobet (Fra)	-22.19			
	KoM Louison Bobet (Fra)				
	TEAM Belgium				
	Starters 116				
	Finishers 51				
1951	**1.** Hugo Koblet (Swi)	142.20.14	32.7	24	4,697
	2. Raphaël Geminiani (Fra)	-22.00			
	3. Lucien Lazaridès (Fra)	-24.16			
	KoM Raphaël Geminiani (Fra)				
	TEAM France				
	Starters 123				
	Finishers 66				

YEAR	RIDERS ON THE PODIUM	TIME	AVG SPD	STAGES	KMS
1952	**1.** Fausto Coppi (Ita)	151.57.20	31.8	23	4,827
	2. Constant "Stan" Ockers (Bel)	-28.27			
	3. Bernardo Ruiz (Spa)	-34.38			
	KoM Fausto Coppi (Ita)				
	TEAM Italy				
	Starters 122				
	Finishers 78				
1953	**1.** Louison Bobet (Fra)	129.23.25	34.6	22	4,479
	2. Jean Mallejac (Fra)	-14.18			
	3. Giancarlo Astrua (Ita)	-15.02			
	POINTS Fritz Shaer (Swi)				
	KoM Jesus Lorono (Spa)				
	TEAM Netherlands				
	Starters 120				
	Finishers 76				
1954	**1.** Louison Bobet (Fra)	140.06.50	34.6	23	4,855
	2. Ferdi Kübler (Swi)	-15.49			
	3. Fritz Schaer (Swi)	-21.46			
	POINTS Ferdi Kübler (Swi)				
	KoM Federico Bahamontes (Spa)				
	TEAM Switzerland				
	Starters 110				
	Finishers 69				
1955	**1.** Louison Bobet (Fra)	130.29.26	34.6	22	4,476
	2. Jean Brankart (Bel)	-4.53			
	3. Charly Gaul (Lux)	-11.30			
	POINTS Stan Ockers (Bel)				
	KoM Charly Gaul (Lux)				
	TEAM France				
	Starters 130				
	Finishers 69				
1956	**1.** Roger Walkowiak (Fra)	124.01.16	36.3	22	4,527
	2. Gilbert Bauvin (Fra)	-1.25			
	3. Jan Adriaenssens (Bel)	-3.44			
	POINTS Stan Ockers (Bel)				

YEAR	RIDERS ON THE PODIUM	TIME	AVG SPD	STAGES	KMS
	KoM Charly Gaul (Lux)				
	TEAM Belgium				
	Starters 120				
	Finishers 88				
1957	**1**. Jacques Anquetil (Fra)	135.44.42	34.5	22	4,664
	2. Marc Janssens (Bel)	-14.56			
	3. Adolf Christian (Aut)	-17.20			
	POINTS Jean Forestier (Fra)				
	KOM Gastone Nencini (Ita)				
	TEAM France				
	Starters 120				
	Finishers 56				
1958	**1.** Charly Gaul (Lux)	116.59.05	36.9	24	4,319
	2. Vito Favero (Ita)	-3.10			
	3. Raphaël Geminiani (Fra)	-3.41			
	POINTS Jean Graczyck (Fra)				
	KoM Federico Bahamontes (Spa)				
	TEAM Belgium				
	Starters 120				
	Finishers 78				
1959	**1.** Federico Bahamontes (Spa)	123.46.45	35.4	22	4,358
	2. Henri Anglade (Fra)	-4.01			
	3. Jacques Anquetil (Fra)	-5.05			
	POINTS André Darrigade (Fra)				
	KoM Federico Bahamontes (Spa)				
	TEAM Belgium				
	Starters 120				
	Finishers 65				
1960	**1.** Gastone Nencini (Ita)	112.08.42	37.2	21	4,173
	2. Graziano Battistini (Ita)	-5.02			
	3. Jan Adriaenssens (Bel)	-10.24			
	POINTS Jean Graczyck (Fra)				
	KoM Imerio Massignan (Ita)				
	TEAM France				
	Starters 128				
	Finishers 81				

YEAR	RIDERS ON THE PODIUM	TIME	AVG SPD	STAGES	KMS
1961	**1.** Jacques Anquetil (Fra)	122.01.33	36.3	21	4,394
	2. Guido Carlesi (Ita)	-12.14			
	3. Charly Gaul (Lux)	-12.16			
	POINTS André Darrigade (Fra)				
	KoM Imerio Massignan (Ita)				
	TEAM France				
	Starters 132				
	Finishers 72				
1962	**1.** Jacques Anquetil (Fra)	114.31.54	37.3	22	4,274
	2. Joseph Planckaert (Bel)	-4.59			
	3. Raymond Poulidor (Fra)	-10.24			
	POINTS Rudi Altig (Ger)				
	KoM Federico Bahamontes (Spa)				
	TEAM Saint Raphael-Helyett				
	Starters 149				
	Finishers 94				
1963	**1.** Jacques Anquetil (Fra)	113.30.05	36.5	21	4,141
	2. Federico Bahamontes (Spa)	-3.35			
	3. José Pérez-Francés (Spa)	-10.14			
	POINTS Rik van Looy (Bel)				
	KoM Federico Bahamontes (Spa)				
	TEAM Saint Raphael-Gitane				
	Starters 130				
	Finishers 76				
1964	**1.** Jacques Anquetil (Fra)	127.09.44	35.4	22	4,505
	2. Raymond Poulidor (Fra)	-0.55			
	3. Federico Bahamontes (Spa)	-4.44			
	POINTS Jan Janssen (Ned)				
	KoM Federico Bahamontes (Spa)				
	TEAM Pelforth-Lejeune-Sauvage				
	Starters 132				
	Finishers 81				
1965	**1.** Felice Gimondi (Ita)	116.42.06	35.9	22	4,176
	2. Raymond Poulidor (Fra)	-2.40			
	3. Gianni Motta (Ita)	-9.18			
	POINTS Jan Janssen (Ned)				

YEAR	RIDERS ON THE PODIUM	TIME	AVG SPD	STAGES	KMS
	KoM J Jiminez (Spa)				
	TEAM Kas				
	Starters 130				
	Finishers 96				
1966	**1.** Lucien Aimar (Fra)	**117.34.21**	**36.6**	**22**	**4,329**
	2. Jan Janssen (Ned)	**-1.07**			
	3. Raymond Poulidor (Fra)	**-2.02**			
	POINTS Walter Planckaert (Bel)				
	KoM J Jiminez (Spa)				
	TEAM Kas				
	Starters 130				
	Finishers 82				
1967	**1.** Roger Pingeon (Fra)	**136.53.50**	**34.8**	**22**	**4,780**
	2. Julio Jimenez (Spa)	**-3.40**			
	3. Franco Balmanion (Ita)	**-7.23**			
	POINTS Jan Janssen (Ned)				
	KoM J Jiminez (Spa)				
	TEAM France				
	Starters 130				
	Finishers 88				
1968	**1.** Jan Janssen (Ned)	**133.49.42**	**34.9**	**22**	**4,492**
	2. Herman Vanspringel (Bel)	**-0.38**			
	3. Ferdinand Bracke (Bel)	**-3.03**			
	POINTS Franco Bitossi (Ita)				
	KoM A Gonzalez (Spa)				
	TEAM Spain				
	Starters 110				
	Finishers 63				
1969	**1.** Eddy Merckx (Bel)	**116.16.02**	**35.3**	**22**	**4,117**
	2. Roger Pingeon (Fra)	**-17.54**			
	3. Raymond Poulidor (Fra)	**-22.13**			
	POINTS Eddy Merckx (Bel)				
	KoM Eddy Merckx (Bel)				
	TEAM Faema				
	Starters 130				
	Finishers 86				

YEAR	RIDERS ON THE PODIUM	TIME	AVG SPD	STAGES	KMS
1970	**1.** Eddy Merckx (Bel)	119.31.49	36.5	23	4,369
	2. Joop Zoetemelk (Ned)	-12.41			
	3. Gösta Petterson (Swe)	-15.54			
	POINTS Walter Godefroot (Bel)				
	KoM Eddy Merckx (Bel)				
	TEAM Salvarini				
	Starters 150				
	Finishers 100				
1971	**1.** Eddy Merckx (Bel)	96.45.14	36.9	20	3,608
	2. Joop Zoetemelk (Ned)	-9.51			
	3. Lucien Van Impe (Bel)	-11.056			
	POINTS Eddy Merckx (Bel)				
	KoM Lucien Van Impe (Bel)				
	TEAM Bic				
	Starters 129				
	Finishers 94				
1972	**1.** Eddy Merckx (Bel)	108.17.18	35.5	22	3,846
	2. Felice Gimondi (Ita)	-10.41			
	3. Raymond Poulidor (Fra)	-11.34			
	POINTS Eddy Merckx (Bel)				
	KoM Lucien Van Impe (Bel)				
	TEAM Gan-Mercier				
	Starters 132				
	Finishers 88				
1973	**1.** Luis Ocaña (Spa)	122.25.34	33.4	20	4,140
	2. Bernard Thévenet (Fra)	-15.51			
	3. José Manuel Fuente (Spa)	-17.15			
	POINTS Herman Vanspringel (Bel)				
	KoM Pedro Torres (Spa)				
	TEAM Bic				
	Starters 132				
	Finishers 88				
1974	**1.** Eddy Merckx (Bel)	116.16.58	35.2	22	4,098
	2. Raymond Poulidor (Fra)	-8.04			
	3. Vicente Lopez-Carrill (Spa)	-8.09			
	POINTS Patrick Sercu (Fra)				

YEAR	RIDERS ON THE PODIUM	TIME	AVG SPD	STAGES	KMS
	KoM Domingo Perurena (Spa)				
	TEAM Kas				
	Starters 130				
	Finishers 105				
1975	**1.** Bernard Thévenet (Fra)	114.35.31	34.9	22	4,000
	2. Eddy Merckx (Bel)	-2.47			
	3. Lucien Van Impe (Bel)	-5.01			
	POINTS Rik van Linden (Bel)				
	KoM Lucien Van Impe (Bel)				
	BYR Francesco Moser (Ita)				
	TEAM Gan-Mercier				
	Starters 140				
	Finishers 83				
1976	**1.** Lucien Van Impe (Bel)	116.22.23	34.5	22	4,017
	2. Joop Zoetemelk (Ned)	-4.14			
	3. Raymond Poulidor (Fra)	-12.08			
	POINTS Freddy Maertens (Bel)				
	KoM G Bellini (Ita)				
	BYR Enrique Martinez-Heredia (Spa)				
	TEAM Kas				
	Starters 130				
	Finishers 87				
1977	**1.** Bernard Thévenet (Fra)	115.38.30	35.4	22	4,096
	2. Hennie Kuiper (Ned)	-0.48			
	3. Lucien Van Impe (Bel)	-3.32			
	POINTS Jean Escalssan (Fra)				
	KoM Lucien Van Impe (Bel)				
	BYR Dietrich Thurau (Ger)				
	TEAM TI-Raleigh				
	Starters 100				
	Finishers 53				
1978	**1.** Bernard Hinault (Fra)	108.18.00	36.0	22	3,908
	2. Joop Zoetemelk (Ned)	-3.56			
	3. Joaquim Agostinho (Por)	-6.54			
	POINTS Freddy Maertens (Bel)				
	KoM Mariano Martinez (Fra)				

YEAR	RIDERS ON THE PODIUM	TIME	AVG SPD	STAGES	KMS
	BYR Henk Lubberding (Ned)				
	TEAM Miko-Mercier				
	Starters 110				
	Finishers 78				
1979	**1.** Bernard Hinault (Fra)	**103.06.50**	**36.5**	**24**	**3,765**
	2. Joop Zoetemelk (Ned)	**-3.07**			
	3. Joaquim Agostinho (Por)	**-26.53**			
	POINTS Bernard Hinault (Fra)				
	KoM Giovanni Battaglin (Ita)				
	BYR Jean-René Bernaudeau (Fra)				
	TEAM Renault				
	Starters 150				
	Finishers 90				
1980	**1.** Joop Zoetemelk (Ned)	**109.19.14**	**35.7**	**22**	**3,842**
	2. Hennie Kuiper (Ned)	**-6.55**			
	3. Raymond Martin (Fra)	**-7.56**			
	POINTS Rudy Pevange (Bel)				
	KoM Raymond Martin (Fra)				
	BYR Johan Van De Velde (Ned)				
	TEAM Miko-Mercier				
	Starters 130				
	Finishers 85				
1981	**1.** Bernard Hinault (Fra)	**96.19.38**	**37.8**	**24**	**3,758**
	2. Lucien Van Impe (Bel)	**-14.34**			
	3. Robert Alban (Fra)	**-17.04**			
	POINTS Freddy Maertens (Bel)				
	KoM Lucien Van Impe (Bel)				
	BYR Peter Winnen (Ned)				
	TEAM Peugot				
	Starters 150				
	Finishers 121				
1982	**1.** Bernard Hinault (Fra)	**93.43.44**	**37.5**	**21**	**3,507**
	2. Joop Zoetemelk (Ned)	**-6.21**			
	3. Jo Van der Velde (Ned)	**-8.59**			
	POINTS Sean Kelly (Ire)				
	KoM B Vallet (Fra)				

YEAR	RIDERS ON THE PODIUM	TIME	AVG SPD	STAGES	KMS
	BYR Phil Anderson (Aus)				
	TEAM Coop-Mercier				
	Starters 189				
	Finishers 125				
1983	**1.** Laurent Fignon (Fra)	107.31.58	36.2	22	3,860
	2. Angel Arroyo (Spa)	-4.04			
	3. Peter Winnen (Ned)	-4.09			
	POINTS Sean Kelly (Ire)				
	KoM Lucien Van Impe (Bel)				
	BYR Laurent Fignon (Fra)				
	TEAM Peugot				
	Starters 140				
	Finishers 88				
1984	**1.** Laurent Fignon (Fra)	112.03.40	34.9	23	4,021
	2. Bernard Hinault (Fra)	-10.32			
	3. Greg LeMond (USA)	-11.46			
	POINTS Frank Hoste (Bel)				
	KoM Robert Miller (GB)				
	BYR Greg LeMond (USA)				
	TEAM Renault				
	Starters 170				
	Finishers 124				
1985	**1.** Bernard Hinault (Fra)	113.24.23	36.2	22	4,109
	2. Greg LeMond (USA)	-1.42			
	3. Stephen Roche (Ire)	-4.29			
	POINTS Sean Kelly (Ire)				
	KoM Luis Herrera (Col)				
	BYR Fabio Parra (Col)				
	TEAM La Vie Claire				
	Starters 180				
	Finishers 144				
1986	**1.** Greg LeMond (USA)	110.35.19	37.0	23	4,084
	2. Bernard Hinault (Fra)	-3.10			
	3. Urs Zimmerman (Swi)	-10.54			
	POINTS Eric Vanderaerden (Bel)				
	KoM Bernard Hinault (Fra)				

YEAR	RIDERS ON THE PODIUM	TIME	AVG SPD	STAGES	KMS
	BYR Andy Hampsten (USA)				
	TEAM La Vie Claire				
	Starters 210				
	Finishers 132				
1987	**1.** Stephen Roche (Ire)	115.27.42	36.6	25	4,331
	2. Pedro Delgado (Spa)	-0.40			
	3. Jean-François Bernard (Fra)	-2.13			
	POINTS Jean-Paul Van Poppel (Ned)				
	KoM Luis Herrera (Col)				
	BYR Raul Alcala (Mex)				
	TEAM Systeme U				
	Starters 207				
	Finishers 135				
1988	**1.** Pedro Delgado (Spa)	84.27.53	39.9	22	3,286
	2. Steven Rooks (Ned)	-7.13			
	3. Fabio Parra (Col)	-9.58			
	POINTS Eddy Planckaert (Bel)				
	KoM Steven Rooks (Ned)				
	BYR Eric Breukink (Ned)				
	TEAM PDM				
	Starters 198				
	Finishers 151				
1989	**1.** Greg LeMond (USA)	87.38.35	37.5	21	4,021
	2. Laurent Fignon (Fra)	-0.08			
	3. Pedro Delgado (Spa)	-3.34			
	POINTS Sean Kelly (Ire)				
	KoM Gert-Jan Theunisse (Ned)				
	BYR not awarded				
	TEAM PDM				
	Starters 198				
	Finishers 138				
1990	**1.** Greg LeMond (USA)	90.43.20	38.6	21	3,504
	2. Claudio Chiapucci (Ita)	-2.16			
	3. Erik Breukink (Ned)	-2.29			
	POINTS Olaf Ludwig (Ger)				
	KoM Thierry Claveyrolat (Fra)				

YEAR	RIDERS ON THE PODIUM	TIME	AVG SPD	STAGES	KMS
	BYR Gilles Delion (Fra)				
	TEAM Z				
	Starters 198				
	Finishers 156				
1991	**1.** Miguel Induráin (Spa)	101.01.20	38.7	22	3,914
	2. Gianni Bugno (Ita)	-3.36			
	3. Claudio Chiapucci (Ita)	-5.56			
	POINTS Djamolodin Abduzhaparov (Uzb)				
	KoM Claudio Chiapucci (Ita)				
	BYR Alvaro Meija (Col)				
	TEAM Banesto				
	Starters 198				
	Finishers 158				
1992	**1.** Miguel Induráin (Spa)	100.49.30	36.5	22	3,983
	2. Claudio Chiapucci (Ita)	-4.35			
	3. Gianni Bugno (Ita)	-10.49			
	POINTS Laurent Jalabert (Fra)				
	KoM Claudio Chiapucci (Ita)				
	BYR Eddy Bouwmans (Ned)				
	TEAM Carrera				
	Starters 198				
	Finishers 130				
1993	**1.** Miguel Induráin (Spa)	95.57.09	38.7	20	3720
	2. Tony Rominger (Swi)	-4.59			
	3. Zenon Jaskula (Pol)	- 5.48			
	POINTS Djamolodin Abduzhaparov (Uzb)				
	KoM Tony Rominger (Swi)				
	BYR Antonio Martin (Spa)				
	TEAM Carrera				
	Starters 180				
	Finishers 136				
1994	**1.** Miguel Induráin (Spa)	103.38.38	38.4	21	3,978
	2. Pietr Ugrumov (Rus)	-5.39			

YEAR	RIDERS ON THE PODIUM	TIME	AVG SPD	STAGES	KMS
	3. Marco Pantani (Ita)	-7.19			
	POINTS Djamolodin Abduzhaparov (Uzb)				
	KoM Richard Virenque (Fra)				
	BYR Marco Pantani (Ita)				
	TEAM Festina				
	Starters 189				
	Finishers 117				
1995	**1.** Miguel Induráin (Spa)	92.44.59	39.2	21	3,635
	2. Alex Zülle (Swi)	-4.35			
	3. Bjarne Riis (Den)	-6.47			
	POINTS Laurent Jalabert (Fra)				
	KoM Richard Virenque (Fra)				
	BYR Marco Pantani (Ita)				
	TEAM ONCE				
	Starters 189				
	Finishers 115				
1996	**1.** Bjarne Riis (Den)	95.57.16	39.2	21	3,765
	2. Jan Ullrich (Ger)	-1.41			
	3. Richard Virenque (Fra)	-4.37			
	POINTS Erik Zabel (Ger)				
	KoM Richard Virenque (Fra)				
	BYR Jan Ullrich (Ger)				
	TEAM Festina				
	Starters 198				
	Finishers 139				
1997	**1.** Jan Ullrich (Ger)	100.30.35	39.2	21	3,950
	2. Richard Virenque (Fra)	-9.09			
	3. Marco Pantani (Ita)	-14.03			
	POINTS Erik Zabel (Ger)				
	KoM Richard Virenque (Fra)				
	BYR Jan Ullrich (Ger)				
	TEAM Team Deutsche Telekom				
	Starters 219				
	Finishers 129				

YEAR	RIDERS ON THE PODIUM	TIME	AVG SPD	STAGES	KMS
1998	**1.** Marco Pantani (Ita)	92.49.46	39.9	21	3,875
	2. Jan Ullrich (Ger)	-3.21			
	3. Bobby Julich (USA)	-4.08			
	POINTS Erik Zabel (Ger)				
	KoM Christophe Rinero (Fra)				
	BYR Jan Ullrich (Ger)				
	TEAM Cofidis				
	Starters 189				
	Finishers 96				
1999	**1.** Lance Armstrong (USA)	91.32.16	40.3	20	3,687
	2. Alex Zülle (Swi)	-7.37			
	3. Fernando Escartín (Spa)	-10.26			
	POINTS Erik Zabel (Ger)				
	KoM Richard Virenque (Fra)				
	BYR Benoit Salmon (Fra)				
	TEAM Banesto				
	Starters 180				
	Finishers 141				
2000	**1.** Lance Armstrong (USA)	92.33.08	39.5	21	3,662
	2. Jan Ullrich (Ger)	-6.02			
	3. Joseba Beloki (Spa)	-10.04			
	POINTS Erik Zabel (Ger)				
	KoM Santiago Botero (Col)				
	BYR Francesco Mancebo (Spa)				
	TEAM Kelme-Costa Blanca				
	Starters 180				
	Finishers 121				
2001	**1.** Lance Armstrong (USA)	86.17.28	40.02	20	3,453
	2. Jan Ullrich (Ger)	-6.44			
	3. Joseba Beloki (Spa)	-9.05			
	POINTS Erik Zabel (Ger)				
	KoM Laurent Jalabert (Fra)				
	BYR Oscar Sevilla (Spa)				
	TEAM Kelme-Costa Blanca				
	Starters 189				
	Finishers 144				

YEAR	RIDERS ON THE PODIUM	TIME	AVG SPD	STAGES	KMS
2002	**1.** Lance Armstrong (USA)	82.05.12	39.9	20	3,276
	2. Joseba Beloki (Spa)	-7.17			
	3. Raymondas Rumsas (Ltu)	-8.17			
	POINTS Robbie McEwen (Aus)				
	KoM Laurent Jalabert (Fra)				
	BYR Ivan Basso (Ita)				
	TEAM ONCE-Eroski				
	Starters 189				
	Finishers 153				
2003	**1.** Lance Armstrong (USA)	83.41.12	40.94	20	3,361
	2. Jan Ullrich (Ger)	-1.01			
	3. Alexandre Vinokourov (Kaz)	-4.14			
	POINTS Baden Cooke (Aus)				
	KoM Richard Virenque (Fra)				
	BYR Denis Menchov (Rus)				
	TEAM Team CSC				
	Starters 189				
	Finishers 147				
2004	**1.** Lance Armstrong (USA)	83.36.02	40.56	20	3,391
	2. Andreas Klöden (Ger)	-6.19			
	3. Ivan Basso (Ita)	-6.40			
	POINTS Robbie McEwen (Aus)				
	KoM Richard Virenque (Fra)				
	BYR Vladimir Karpets (Rus)				
	TEAM T-Mobile				
	TEAM T-Mobile				
	Starters 188				
	Finishers 147				
2005	**1.** Lance Armstrong (USA)	86.15.02	41.654		3,608
	2. Ivan Basso (Ita)	-4:40			
	3. Jan Ullrich (Ger)	-6:21			
	POINTS Thor Hushovd (Nor)				
	KoM Michael Rasmussen (Den)				
	BYR Yaroslav Popovych (Ukr)				
	TEAM T-Mobile				
	Starters 189				
	Finishers 155				

Appendix C

RESOURCE GUIDE

Recommended Reading

Abt, Samuel. *Off to the Races: 25 Years of Cycling Journalism*. Boulder, CO: Velo Press, 2002.

Dauncey, Hugh, and Geoff Hare, eds. *The Tour de France 1903–2003: A Century of Sporting Structures, Meanings and Values*. Portland, OR: Frank Cass Publishers, 2003.

Fife, Graeme. *Inside the Peloton: Riding, Winning & Losing the Tour de France*. Edinburgh, Scotland: Mainstream Publishing, 2001.

Prehn, Thomas. *Racing Tactics for Cyclists*. Boulder, CO: Velo Press, 2004.

Wilcockson, John. *23 Days in July: Inside the Tour de France and Lance Armstrong's Record-Breaking Victory*. Cambridge, MA: Da Capo Press, 2005.

Woodland, Les. *The Unknown Tour de France: The Many Faces of the World's Biggest Bicycle Race*. San Francisco: Van Der Plas Publications, 2000.

Of Interest on the Web

Le Tour de France: Official Website—www.letour.fr (English version available)

Velo News—www.velonews.com

Cyclingnews.com—www.cyclingnews.com

Bicycling magazine's TdF—www.tourdefrancenews.com

Pez Cycling News—www.pezccyclingnews.com

Outdoor Life Network—www.olntv.com

TdF Blog—www.tdfblog.com

Lance Armstrong Official Fan Club—www.thepaceline.com

Torelli's Tour de France History—www.torelli.com/raceinfo/tdf/tdfhistory.shtml

J. P. Partland has been writing about cycling since 1991, covering some of the sport's biggest races. He has been published in nearly every cycling magazine as well as many mainstream publications. He is the author of two books on cycling: *Mountain Bike Madness* and *The World of BMX*. He also has medalled at the U.S. National Championships and raced the Irish Milk Ras, Ireland's version of the Tour.

"*Tour Fever* is an insightful look at the world's greatest bike race, the Tour de France. It educates the novice while providing cutting-edge information and reference for the seasoned professional."

—Tom Danielson, Discovery Channel Professional Cycling Team member

"*Tour Fever* is the perfect title for a book so full of factual information about the world's greatest bike race. But it is also a highly entertaining read, which will amuse the armchair fan for weeks on end—for the whole of July perhaps . . ."

—Graham Watson, Tour de France photographer and author

"*Tour Fever* is like a textbook about how the Tour de France operates. I was amazed at how it covered everything from the current racing scene to the history of the Tour de France."

—Frankie Andreu, nine-time Tour de France competitor, captain of the 1999 and 2000 Tour de France–winning United States Postal Service team

"J.P. does a great job of capturing the majesty, drama and exuberance of Tour fever. It's easy to recommend the book for experienced and novice cyclists alike, but the book's greatest strength may be its ability to explain the race to a non-cyclist. It is the only book I would recommend to a cyclist's partner. And for anyone wanting to share their loved one's excitement, I can't recommend the book highly enough."

—Patrick Brady, publisher, *Asphalt Magazine*